PILANESBERG
GUIDE

Leopard
Panthera pardus

PILANESBERG NATIONAL PARK – Facilities Grid

NAME	CONTACT NUMBER	Game Drives	Game Walks	Bush Braais	Conferences	Disabled Facilities	Curio Shop	Restaurant	Pool	Camping	Self-catering Chalets	Hotel	COMMENTS
North West Parks Board	(014) 555-5351/2/3/4												Responsible for biodiversity conservation and tourism management
Manyane	(014) 555-6135/6	•	•		•	•	•	•	•	•	•		Caravan park, putt-putt course and aviary
Bakgatla	(014) 555-6135/6	•	•		•			•	•		•		Children's playground
Tshukudu	(014) 552-6255	•	•										Own waterhole
Bakubung	(014) 552-6000	•	•	•	•	•	•	•	•		•	•	Timeshare and hotel
Kwa Maritane	(014) 552-5100	•	•	•	•	•	•	•	•		•	•	Timeshare and hotel
	(014) 552-5020	•	•	•	•								Also do balloon safaris www.gametrac.co.za
Mankwe Safaris	(014) 555-7056 082 415 2338	•		•		•							Specialise in heritage drives with particular focus on the Ba-Tswana culture
Pilanesberg Centre	083 4412001 083 4539558				•			•	•				Stunning view, sweets, refreshments and clean toilets

Acknowledgements

North West Parks: Steve Johnson, Hector Magome, Johnson Maoka, Koos Herbst, Bruce Brocket, Phil Johnson, Lowain Van Velden, Gus van Dyke, Les Ashley, Greg Stuart-Hill, Moses Mothusi, Bernard Marobe, Wilf Slade, Doc Shongwe

Goldfields Education Centre: Matlhomola Molwantwa; Billy Leketi; Rapula Ratsoga; Kenny Ditsi, Mac Magodielo; Moremi Lesejane; Moses Thebe

Text Development: Keryn Adcock, Dave Gear (Saint Stithian's College), Dr. John Bristow (Minerals and Energy Policy Centre), Professor Grant Cawthorn (Wits Geological Dept), Simon Hall (Wits Archaeology Dept), Francois Coetzee (UNISA Archaeology Dept), Ria Milburn(Bush Education Safaris)

Map Developement: Metro GIS

Design and DTP Origination: Jacana

Photography: Paul Funston, Gus van Dyk, Gary van der Merwe

Historical artwork and photographs: Daniell, S. 1820a *African scenery and animals* 1804-1805. London: S Daniell. (Reprint by Balkema, Rotterdam.); Frescura, F. 1981. *Rural Shelter in Southern Africa.* Johannesburg: Ravan; Hardie G.J. 1981. *Tswana, design of house and settlement - Continuity and change in expressive space.* Boston: Boston University, Graduate School.

Translations: Ephraim Morei, T J Matebesi

Special thanks: Clive Webber (Johannesburg College of Education), Gert Brummer (GBD), Glynis & Alistair Clacherty (Clacherty & Ass), Joe Moser (Makanyane Volunteers), Chris Lee (Friends of Pilanesberg), Rick Matthews, Satellite Applications Centre, Frieda Kilian and the reviewers

CONTENTS

Vervet Monkeys
(page 21)

VOLCANOES AND ROCKS

It is 1 300 million years ago. Primitive organisms like algae are the only life-form on earth. It is a hostile place. Strong winds howl, earthquakes and huge volcanic eruptions are common.

BIRTH OF PILANESBERG

Pilanesberg is one of the largest volcanic complexes of its kind in the world. The rare rock types and structure of the Pilanesberg make it a unique geological feature.

These four pages will take you back into time, to Pilanesberg's violent birth millions of years ago. They explain how it happened, and what you can see today as you drive through the Park.

A
Tearing the Earth apart

The furnace inside the earth is hotter than 1 000°C and has caused rocks to melt. This molten rock (magma) floods up the cracks the earthquake has caused. The magma collects in a large pool, called a 'hot spot', just below the crust. It builds up immense pressure against the roof of the magma chamber (arrows show direction of flowing magma).

B Cracks release the fire

This pressure stretches deep circular and radial cracks to split the earth's crust open. When viewed from above, these cracks look like a window that has been hit by a stone (See Satellite photo, page 4). Boiling rock, ash and gas erupt violently into the sky. The rocks at G1 (see page 5 and Map, page 64) are from the initial explosions. They are called volcanic rocks.

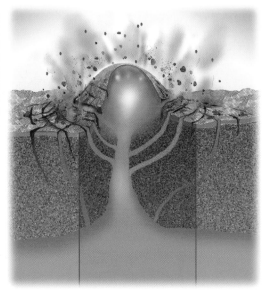

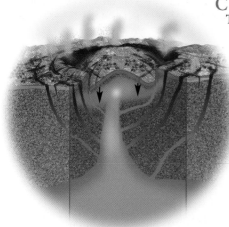

C
The crust collapses
When the magma bursts out of its holding chamber, there is no longer any support for the brittle, stretched crust above it. As a result, the crust collapses down into the magma chamber (arrows show direction of crust collapsing).

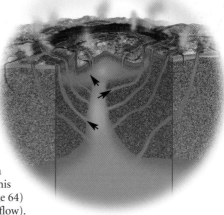

D
Lava flows out
When the crust collapses, magma that is still in the chamber is forced upwards. This process is the same as when a cork is pushed into a full bottle of liquid and the liquid and air spurt out. Magma pours out of the cracks and floods the landscape as lava. This lava solidifies into volcanic rocks and remnants of this can be seen at G3 (see page 5 and Map, page 64) (arrows show direction of lava flow).

E
Magma cools and clogs up the cracks
Some magma does not erupt onto the surface as lava. It begins to cool, harden and clog up the cracks inside the Earth. It then solidifies into rock formations known as dykes. They consist of rocks called foyaites and syenites. In Pilanesberg, many of these dykes are circular in shape because of the circular cracks, and are called ring-dykes. They are especially prominent in the south-west of Pilanesberg. (See Satellite Photo, page 4).

The entire process happened many times during the volcano's active lifespan of about 1 million years. Each time a new set of cracks opens up, different types of magma are released. Different rock types are formed in this way.

Eventually the volcano settles down and time and erosion take over to shape the land into what we see today.

VOLCANOES AND ROCKS

Erosion has exposed the inside of the original volcano and its rocks to us. Today we see what is left after millions of years of weathering.

For the key to the map colours, see the opposite page.

Major rock types the Park today
Cross Section (indicated by _ _ _ _)
from Sun City (**A**) through Mankwe Dam (**B**) to Manyane (**C**)

Volcanic rocks (lavas & tuffs) erode much faster than the ring-dykes and outcrops of foyaite and syenite. As a result these erosion-resistant syenites and foyaites stand out prominently.

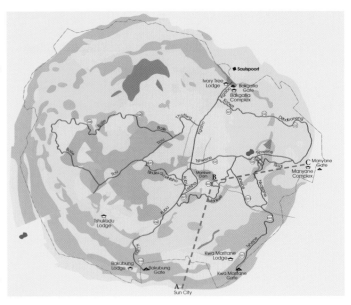

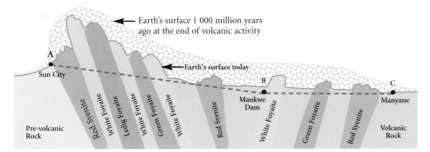

Cross section showing: A Sun City, Pre-volcanic Rock, Red Syenite, White Foyaite, Ledig Foyaite, White Foyaite, Green Foyaite, White Foyaite, Red Syenite, B Mankwe Dam, White Foyaite, Green Foyaite, Red Syenite, C Manyane, Volcanic Rock. Earth's surface 1 000 million years ago at the end of volcanic activity. Earth's surface today.

Satellite photo

This satellite photo shows the ring-dyke structure which is more noticeable in the south-west of the complex. It also shows the central rocky outcrops and flatter regions of volcanic rock in the north-east. Millions of years after the volcanic explosions, a crack in the earth's crust cut the Pilanesberg in half, from the south-west to the north-east. Erosion took advantage of this weakness and eventually formed a broad valley across Pilanesberg. Tlou Drive follows some of this eroded fault zone.

Pilanesberg has survived aeons of erosion, and stands high above the surrounding bushveld plains. Near the centre stands Thabayadiotso, which is a fitting name, meaning the 'proud mountain'.

The turbulence which formed Pilanesberg has moved away long ago, due to the shifting of the earth's continents. For this reason we can be almost sure that Pilanesberg will never erupt again. But the process of erosion continues and so do the cycles of nature in Pilanesberg.

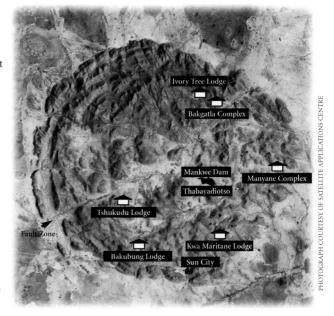

Key to Geological Sites

These sites are marked on the Map on pages 64 and 65.

Number marked on route in Park	Geological Sites	Cut and polished rock surfaces	Key to map on opposite page
	Man-made		
G8	**Old Flourite Mine** – The old Moepo mine can be seen up against the mountain, where purple fluorite, containing calcium and fluorine, was mined. Minerals soaked into the rocks in the same way as G13.		
	90 million years old		
G4	**Kimberlite** – In the 1920s a prospector discovered this Kimberlite pipe. The bright red garnets he found could have indicated diamonds; but he had no luck!		
	1 300 million years old		
G1	**Volcanic Rocks** **Volcanic Tuff** – 1 300 million years ago a volcanic eruption blasted massive rocks, kilometers into the sky. The biggest boulders fell back to earth first; smaller ones scattered above them. A series of blasts, over time, created layers of these rocks, called tuffs, exposed now by erosion.		
G3	**Lava** – As lava flowed on the earth's surface, it cooled rapidly through exposure to air and wind.		
G13	**Uranium-bearing Tuff** – Mildly radio active tuffs due to uranium content. The minerals inside are a result of super-heated water (200-400°C) which soaked into the rock at the end of the volcanoes' active life. The rock continues for kms underground, sometimes exposed through erosion.		
G6	**Foyaites** **Green** – In the surging sea of magma, deep below the earths' surface, many minerals were carried upwards. As the magma cooled they became set into rock. One, aegerine, grew in a needle-like form in this foyaite.		
G10	**Green** – Nepheline in this rock dissolves easily resulting in a pitted surface typical of foyaites.		
G5	**White** – Surrounding hills are coarse-grained rock that crystallised slowly from molten magma inside the earth. It is rich in feldspar, nepheline and zirconium.		
G14	**White** – Foyaites are not easily weathered, so the hills in this area are prominent.		
G9	**Red** – This area is underlain by white foyaite. Red foyaite was created when super-heated water altered the composition and colour of the rock, by soaking it with red iron oxide.		
G15	**Red** – Approximate geographic centre of the volcano with multiple, parallel bands of red syenite and red foyaite, created over a million years ago from magma. The site is underwater many months of the year.		
G11	**Ledig** – Contains small, unharmful amounts of uranium, as well as aegerine (magnesium, iron, sodium and silica). Also formed from magma.		
	Tinguite – This has no geological site on the Map.		
G7	**Syenites** **Red** – Makes good polished facing stone. 20 years ago attempts to quarry it failed as it contains grains of iron oxide that do not polish well. On the hill behind, long, vertical, drilling holes can be seen.		
G12	**Red** – Largely composed of potassium-rich orthoclase, feldspar, chlorite (iron, magnesium, silica and water), calcium and fluorine. Syenite is igneous rock, formed from magma.		
G2	**Nepheline** – Formed when boiling magma rose to just below the earth's surface, then cooled down rapidly and solidified. White feldspar crystals were captured in the direction of the flowing magma.		
	2 000 million years old		
	Pre-volcanic rocks **Granite and Gabbro** – These have no geological site on the Map.		

FORMATION OF HABITATS

Once the volcano stopped blasting the area into new shape, time slowly started transforming Pilanesberg, and life settled down in this natural sanctuary. The forces of nature gradually changed the landscape and created the habitats we see today. Man-made areas have also been created – dams are now the lifeblood of the Park, and roads have attracted many specific species. The formation of natural and man-made habitats is a never-ending process.

HILLSIDE AND GRASSLAND

Hillside vegetation differs from grassland because the gradient of the slope allows nutrients in the soil to drain to the bottom of the slope.

Different soils and the effects of fire also change the vegetation. Grass has relatively little moisture content, and so grassland attracts species which are more dependent on drinking regularly.

Rain
Water from heavy rainstorms washes soil downhill. Natural erosion is caused, especially on the steeper slopes, where faster flowing water carries away large amounts of soil.

South-facing Slopes
Southern slopes are cooler and retain moisture, as they receive less sun. Typical trees found here include the Weeping Faurea and the Common Cabbage-tree.
(See pages 51 & 55)

Flowing water causes nutrients and soil to drain to the bottom of slopes.

Ouklip
Over decades, as the water from waterlogged areas evaporates, iron-rich minerals are left behind. These bake in the heat of summer. Eventually a hard layer of rock, called ouklip, is formed beneath a layer of top soil. Trees struggle to take root through the hard ouklip layer, but grassland flourishes.

Ouklip

Sweetveld
These lower lying areas becom waterlogged in summer resulting the growth of sweetveld. Graze prefer sweetveld, and it is often o grazed. Many species therefore m onto hillslopes in winter.

6

Sun

Large rocks are broken down
by centuries of weathering.
Gravity carries them
down the slope.

North-facing Slopes
North-facing slopes receive
more sun. They are hotter
and drier, and have different
vegetation from southern
slopes. Typical trees found
here are Live-long Lannea
and Red Bushwillow.
(See pages 46 & 47)

On grassland, zebra,
wildebeest and tsessebe,
evolved in larger herds as
grassland provides more food per
hectare than any other habitat and
can sustain large numbers of
animals. These animals also rely on
safety in numbers, as it is harder
for predators to pick out a single
animal. They developed speed and
stamina to outrun predators on
the open areas.

Over thousands of years the rocks are
worn down to form soil. These
nutrients in the soil feed the
plants, which in turn
feed the animals.

Two species graze here in smaller
groups – the White Rhino which
lacks speed, but is successful due to
its size and strength, and the hippo,
which grazes at night.

Formation of Habitats (continued)

Thickets

Thickets provide less food per hectare than grassland. Small groups of browsers that enjoy leaves, thorns, fruit, pods and bark, feed here. Many animals rely on the dense cover of thickets for protection, as well as on camouflage and agility. Small herds can keep together in thickets, even when chased by predators.

Thickets offer safety for mothers and their young. Many species, including the big cats, give birth to young in thickets, keeping them there until they are strong enough to move into more open areas.

Gully Thickets

Erosion wears away gullies and kloofs between hillslopes. These areas are sheltered from the sun and are therefore usually cooler and wetter.

This gives protection against fire and allows dense vegetation to grow. Gully thickets are remnants of ancient forests which have survived dry periods due to the shade, protection and greater moisture there.

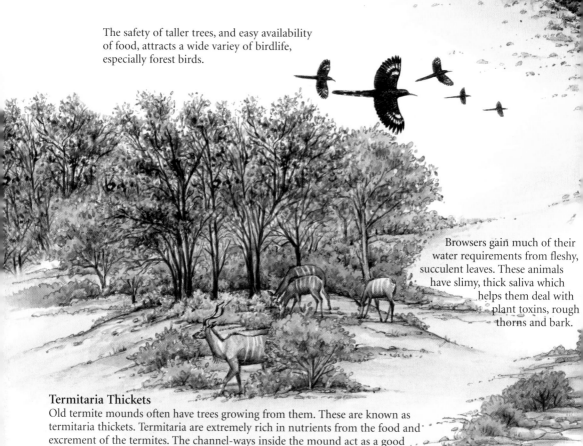

The safety of taller trees, and easy availability of food, attracts a wide variey of birdlife, especially forest birds.

Browsers gain much of their water requirements from fleshy, succulent leaves. These animals have slimy, thick saliva which helps them deal with plant toxins, rough thorns and bark.

Termitaria Thickets

Old termite mounds often have trees growing from them. These are known as termitaria thickets. Termitaria are extremely rich in nutrients from the food and excrement of the termites. The channel-ways inside the mound act as a good reservoir for water. Seeds are carried in by wind or birds. The rich, moist soil enables seeds to take root easily here.

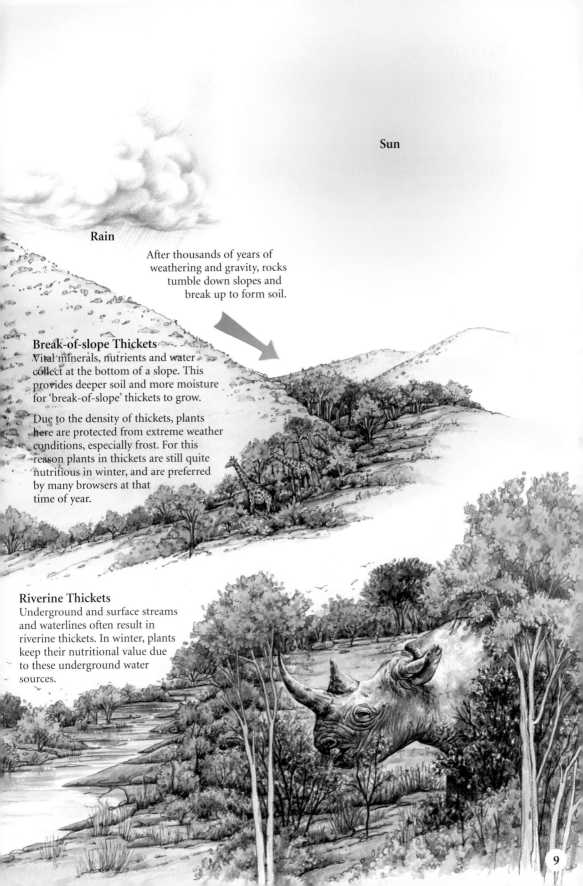

Sun

Rain

After thousands of years of weathering and gravity, rocks tumble down slopes and break up to form soil.

Break-of-slope Thickets

Vital minerals, nutrients and water collect at the bottom of a slope. This provides deeper soil and more moisture for 'break-of-slope' thickets to grow.

Due to the density of thickets, plants here are protected from extreme weather conditions, especially frost. For this reason plants in thickets are still quite nutritious in winter, and are preferred by many browsers at that time of year.

Riverine Thickets

Underground and surface streams and waterlines often result in riverine thickets. In winter, plants keep their nutritional value due to these underground water sources.

FORMATION OF HABITATS (CONTINUED)

ROCKY AREAS

Rocky outcrops in the Park consist mainly of foyaites and syenites. These rocks are harder than most, and therefore do not erode as quickly as other rocks. As a result, Pilanesberg's rocky outcrops stand out prominently. Species, like the klipspringer and leopard, have adapted to this specialised habitat.

Wind, rain, sun, fire and chemical action erode rocks over centuries. This weathering, as well as the force of gravity, eventually loosens large boulders. They tumble down, break up and finally become soil.

Soil, water and minerals flow between rocks, and collect in basins and pockets along the way. At first pioneer plants grow, improving soil conditions. Decaying matter from these plants enriches the soil, so that other more permanent species can grow, later on.

Animals in rocky areas are able to climb and jump well. Unlike plain's animals, they are not built for speed. They take advantage of the height and the rocks to avoid predators. Rocks absorb heat in the day and give off warmth at night. Reptiles bask on warm rocks to regulate body temperature.

Seeds blown by wind, or carried by birds or animals, come to rest in these fertile, moist pockets of soil. Rocky areas also create favourable conditions for plants to grow by being well sheltered and less susceptable to fire.

Bushveld Red-balloon seed-pod (see page 53 and Map; Point 16)

Caves and crevices provide excellent shelter and protection from danger.

Most animals that live in rocky areas do not depend on daily water. Their food provides them with enough moisture.

All streams and rivers in Pilanesberg, arise within the Park itself. They are therefore pollution-free. No rivers here are perennial, and they flow only in a wet summer when they refill dams.

Man-made habitats have also attracted certain animals and plants.

Dams have given Pilanesberg water all year round, and have provided visitors with attractive viewing sites.

Roads are used by many species, and they allow visitors to view nature at close range, without damaging or disturbing it.

Streams from gullies and hillslopes run onto flat areas and natural depressions in the landscape. Some of these natural catchment areas are perfect sites for dams to be built. Dams ensure there is some water during very dry periods.

A smaller dam upstream acts as a filter, preventing the lower dam from silting up. Deposits of silt allow reeds to establish that act as a filter and slow down the flow of water. This helps it to last longer and results in clearer, cleaner water in the lower dam.

Many animals, especially predators like lions, use man-made roads for easier access. They can walk silently here when stalking prey. Roads often stop veld fires from spreading.

Areas with permanent water are well vegetated and attract a diversity of species. Aquatic species live here permanently – crabs, fish and reptiles (like crocodiles and water monitors) and amphibians (like hippos, frogs and terrapins). Dams with islands and dead trees provide safe nesting sites, especially for waterbirds.

Water run-off creates dense hedges of vegetation next to the road. However, due to dust thrown up by cars, this is not regularly browsed. Hedges must be controlled to give better visibility to visitors.

Mammals

Pilanesberg has at least 44 mammal species one can identify while on a game drive. Take note of where each animal is found. You will find each has particular habitat preferences that meet most or all of the animal's requirements.

Species details:
- Height or length are measured in centimetres or metres.
- Height (H) is ground to shoulder.
- Length (L) is tip of nose to tip of tail.
- The Tswana names of the species, where possible, have been written in brackets.

Big Game

All these animals, except buffalo, are described as megaherbivores as their body mass is greater than 1 000 kg. Such large body sizes require a huge amount of food to sustain them. They have very large stomachs to process all the food. Nearly all of them eat grass as this is the most abundant source of food in the system.

The giraffe is the only browser, but because of the height at which it browses, has little competition with other animals. The elephant will switch its diet in the dry season to foraging on woody plant material because of the higher nutritional content.

◄ **White Rhinoceros**
(Tshukudu e Tshweu)
Ceratotherium simum
(1,8 m H)
Heavier than Black Rhino; mouth wide and square; feeds on short grass in open areas; lives in family groups; poor eyesight but acute hearing and smell; when threatened, put their rumps together facing outwards; newborn calf will follow behind mother, but after a few weeks, it will run ahead. In Tswana there is a saying *'Tshukudu kwa gobe e isiwa ke ngwana,'* which means 'children always lead their parents into trouble!'

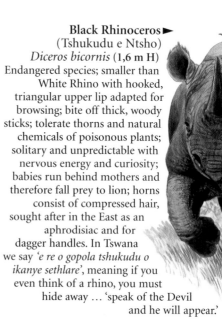

Black Rhinoceros ►
(Tshukudu e Ntsho)
Diceros bicornis **(1,6 m H)**
Endangered species; smaller than White Rhino with hooked, triangular upper lip adapted for browsing; bite off thick, woody sticks; tolerate thorns and natural chemicals of poisonous plants; solitary and unpredictable with nervous energy and curiosity; babies run behind mothers and therefore fall prey to lion; horns consist of compressed hair, sought after in the East as an aphrodisiac and for dagger handles. In Tswana we say *'e re o gopola tshukudu o ikanye sethlare'*, meaning if you even think of a rhino, you must hide away ... 'speak of the Devil and he will appear.'

Dung Beetle ►
(Khukhwane ya boloko)
Family Scarabaeidae (5 - 50 mm)
Dung Beetles frequent rhino middens; adults and larvae eat dung balls; an egg is laid inside ball that is buried by beetle; larvae eaten by genets, civets, birds and baboons, creating a long food chain in nature.

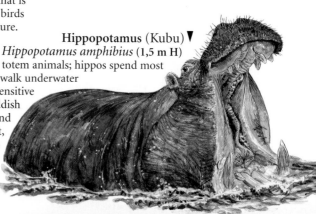

Hippopotamus (Kubu) ▼
Hippopotamus amphibius **(1,5 m H)**
The Bakubung tribe have the hippo as their totem animals; hippos spend most of the day in water; mate, suckle young and walk underwater creating paths that keep waterways open; sensitive skins protected from ultraviolet rays by a reddish oil secretion; highly territorial, they defend pear-shaped home-ranges; graze at night, often covering up to 10 km while eating up to 130 kg of food; responsible for more human fatalities than any other animal in Africa, moving at speeds of 30 km/h.

◄**Elephant** (Tlou)
Loxodonta africana (**3,2 - 4m H**)
Bulls have rounded foreheads whereas cows' are angular; have an acute sense of smell and hearing but limited sight; often a preference for left or right, shown by one tusk being more worn than the other; herds are lead by matriarchs; bulls are solitarily or in bachelor herds; eat about 300 kg of food, and drink about 160 litres of water a day; although they damage trees, this helps create low growth for smaller browsers; visitors must approach with caution, especially breeding herds.

Buffalo (Nare)►
Syncerus caffer (**1,5 m H**)
Introduced from Addo Elephant National Park as they were free of foot and mouth, and Corridor disease; to keep herds healthy, buffalo from other regions will not be introduced; males have large horns with heavier bosses than females; grazers, but browse if grass is scarce; adult bulls often wallow in mud; not territorial, but form large herds with bulls sometimes breaking away into bachelor herds; acute sense of smell; normally docile but old bulls have been known to kill lion; extremely dangerous when wounded.

◄**Giraffe** (Thutlwa)
Giraffa camelopardalis (**3,3 m H**)
Tallest mammal; weighs up to 2 000 kg; browse over 100 tree species, especially thorn-trees; not dependant on daily water; non-territorial, living in loose social system; known to eat bones for extra calcium; despite height it has only seven vertebrae – same number as humans; a special system of valves in the neck prevents excessive blood pressure to head when stooping to drink.

13

PREDATORS

Predators play a fearsome game of competing with each other for food and habitat. Lion are definitely at the top of the hierarchy being the strongest predators. Their social natures also give an added advantage as they can defend their prey and their kills from others.

Cheetah and Wild Dog suffer the most, and survive only by actively avoiding the more powerful predators. They use different habitats and are active in the day when lions are resting. Fortunately for the Brown Hyaena there are no Spotted Hyaena in Pilanesberg – they will steal the Brown Hyaena's prey, harass and even kill them.

Brown Hyaena (Phiri) ▼
Hyaena brunnea (**80 cm H**)
Long mane erected when alarmed, making it look fearsome; scavenger but also hunts small prey, using excellent sense of smell; white droppings characterised by high hair content; territorial males have large home-ranges, marked by scent paste from anal glands. (See Map, Point 24).

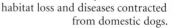

Leopard (Nkwe) ▼
Panthera pardus (**60 cm H**)
Solitary, secretive, nocturnal animals; spend most of the day in hiding; territory is scent-marked with urine; possibly the most dangerous predator when wounded or trapped, using strength, teeth and claws; sacred animal whose tracks can be found at Mankwe Dam ("Place of the Leopard"); only the Kgosi, chief, was allowed to wear the skin.

◄ Wild Dog (Letlhalerwa) ▼
Lycaon pictus (**68 cm H**)
Highly organised social structure in the pack; only dominant male and female mate; whole pack supports pups by regurgitating meat brought back from kills; most endangered carnivores in Africa; require large territories; threatened by stock farmers, habitat loss and diseases contracted from domestic dogs.

◄ African Wild Cat (Phage)
Felis silvestris (**38 cm H**)
Ancestor of the domestic tabby, but larger with longer legs; orange-brown, black-tipped ears; mainly nocturnal; hunt small rodents, terrestrial birds, reptiles, amphibians and insects, as well as larger prey such as dassies, rabbits or even the young of small antelope; mostly solitary except when breeding; threatened by cross-breeding with feral domestic cats.

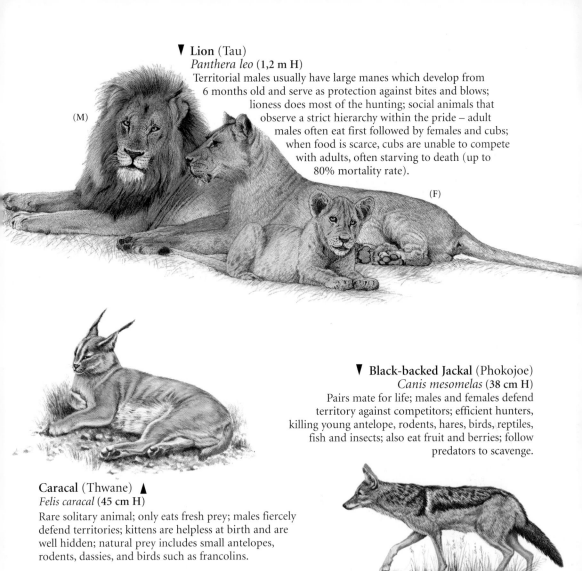

▼ Lion (Tau)
Panthera leo **(1,2 m H)**
Territorial males usually have large manes which develop from 6 months old and serve as protection against bites and blows; lioness does most of the hunting; social animals that observe a strict hierarchy within the pride – adult males often eat first followed by females and cubs; when food is scarce, cubs are unable to compete with adults, often starving to death (up to 80% mortality rate).

(M)

(F)

▼ Black-backed Jackal (Phokojoe)
Canis mesomelas **(38 cm H)**
Pairs mate for life; males and females defend territory against competitors; efficient hunters, killing young antelope, rodents, hares, birds, reptiles, fish and insects; also eat fruit and berries; follow predators to scavenge.

Caracal (Thwane) ▲
Felis caracal **(45 cm H)**
Rare solitary animal; only eats fresh prey; males fiercely defend territories; kittens are helpless at birth and are well hidden; natural prey includes small antelopes, rodents, dassies, and birds such as francolins.

◄ Cheetah (Lengau) ►
Acinonyx jubatus
(80 cm H)
Prefer open country, have keen eyesight for hunting in daylight; sleek, elongated bodies and semi-retractable claws are adaptations for speed; fastest land-mammal on earth with estimated top speed of about 100 km/h; cubs resemble honey badgers, which possibly deters predators.

15

Herbivores

Browsers

Browsing antelope feed on woody plant material, which includes trees and bushes. Because of their diet, you will find these animals associated with woody habitats, such as closed savannah or thicket.

Most of them are ruminants – they chew the cud so they can extract most of the nutrients out of the plant. They also have different mouthparts to grazers. Grazers have broad muzzles for grazing down the grass layer. Browsers have narrower muzzles for selecting and plucking off leaves from the stem. Impala, like the elephant, will graze in the wet season but browse in the dry season.

▲ **Steenbok** (Phudufudu)
Raphicerus campestris (**52 cm H**)
Solitary or in pairs in established territories; depend on water; when threatened, flee in a zig-zag run, then stop to glance back; young hidden for a few weeks; lie motionless when approached; Martial Eagles prey on the young.

◄ **Eland** (Phofu)
Taurotragus oryx (**1,7 m H**)
Largest African antelope; distinctive dewlap on the throat and neck hump; primarily browsers, independent of water, getting moisture from roots, tubers and melons; do not sweat thus saving body water; very agile, can clear 2 m fences; females have been known to chase lion away from their young.

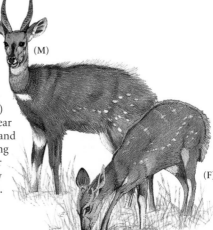

Bushbuck (Serolobotlhoko) ►
Tragelaphus scriptus (**80 cm H**)
Buskbuck browse and graze; found in thickets near water; males are dark brown, females chestnut; shy and mainly nocturnal; solitary animals or in pairs picking up fruit and flowers dropped by monkeys and other tree-dwellers; strong swimmers; move to shallow water if threatened; main enemy is the leopard.

▼ Klipspringer (Kololo)
Oreotragus oreotragus (**60 cm H**)
Live in small family groups; mark territory by dung-piles and pheromone secretion from eye-gland; hooves are blunt with long narrow pads to prevent slipping on rocks; coat has course, hollow, flattened hairs which insulate and help to conserve water; rarely drink water; browse on shrubs, fallen leaves, fruit, flowers and pods.

(M)

▼ Impala (Phala)
Aepyceros melampus (**90 cm H**)
Impala browse and graze; dominant males establish territories and spend rutting season chasing females, grunting and snorting; in breeding season one male dominates breeding herd of females, weaker males group as bachelors; out of season females in nursery herds in loose association with bachelor herds; browse and graze on a wide variety of plants; can jump 3 m high and 12 m in length.

(M)

◄ Springbok (Tshepe)
Antidorcas marsupialis (**75 cm H**)
Springbok browse and graze new grass, flowers and bulbs; occur in herds; well adapted to hot arid regions as not dependent on water; adults 'pronk' when danger threatens (bound around on stiff legs, backs arched); young copy adults to give vent to energy.

▼ Kudu (Tholo)
Tragelaphus strepsiceros (**1,45 m H**)
Male has long, spiralled horns; almost exclusively browsers with excellent hearing; they are agile and can jump 2 m fences from a standing position; hoarse alarm bark is loudest of the antelope.

(M)   (F)

(M)

▲ Common Duiker (Phuti/Photi)
Sylvicapra grimmia (**52 cm H**)
Solitary browsers showing preference for tips of plants; rarely drink water; most active at night or cooler parts of day; rely on keen senses of smell and vision; freeze in danger, flee in ducking, zig-zag manner.

17

Herbivores
(continued)

Grazers

Antelope grazers' diet consists predominantly of grass material. You will find these animals associated with grassland, open savannah or woodland where there is enough food available.

Animals often compete with each other for resources, but will also establish relationships that benefit each other. Wildebeest and zebra are often found together because zebras graze the long, stemmy parts of the grass exposing the green leaves beneath that wildebeest prefer. Zebras benefit because a larger group-size means more eyes are on the look-out for predators. There is also less chance of being the victim to a stalking lion.

▼ **Tsessebe** (Tshesebe)
Damaliscus lunatus (1,3 m H)
White on rump is not as prominent as hartebeest; unlike hartebeest, they drink regularly; grazers, preferring grassy areas surrounded by woodland; regarded as the fastest antelope in southern Africa, reaching speeds of 60 km/h; calves join the herd almost immediately after birth.

◄**Red Hartebeest** (Kgama)
Alcelaphus buselaphus
(1,2 m H)
Conspicuous white patches on rump; can live without water, grazing almost exclusively; when threatened jump stiff-leggedly with all 4 feet off the ground (pronking); very fast animal, can outrun pursuers; mother conceals newborn calf, returning to feed it and eat its faeces and urine which attract predators.

◄ **Common Waterbuck** (Pitlhwa)
Kobus ellipsiprymnus (1,3 m H)
Characteristic white ring on rumps; gregarious grazers, browsing occasionally; use water as refuge, sometimes submerging with only nostrils protruding; oily hair aids waterproofing and has a strong turpentine smell.

(M)

▲ **Sable Antelope** (Kwalata)
Hippotragus niger (1,3 m H)
Adult males are darker and have bigger horns; prefer medium-tall grass, drinking water once a day; males are territorial with some in bachelor herds, while dominant cows lead nursery herds; do not usually mix with other animals, and most game gives way to them at water.

◄ Common Reedbuck
(Mofele o mohibidu/Motlobo)
Redunca arundinum (**90 cm H**)
Rewarding to see as they are shy and
rare; mothers only suckle babies once a
day; baby moves around frequently to
avoid predation; prefer tall grass near
water and will swim in extreme danger;
have sharp alarm whistle, fleeing in
rocking-horse motion with tails fanned
over backs.

(M)

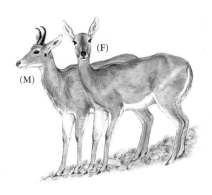

(M)   (F)

▲ Mountain Reedbuck (Mofele wa thaba/
Mofele o Mohibidu)
Redunca fulvorufula (**72 cm H**)
Only male has horns; strictly grazers;
usually occur in groups of 3 - 6; spend
days on rocky slopes, nights on grassy
areas near water; lie close together when
resting; have shrill alarm whistle.

Gemsbok (Kukama) ▼
Oryx gazella (**1,2 m H**)
Graze, but also eat roots, bulbs
and melons for moisture; will
only drink water when
available; sometimes eat the
soil for minerals; white
belly reflects heat from
the bare sand which
helps regulate body
temperature; kidneys
concentrate urine so
only a few drops
are passed.

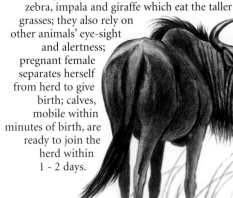

▼ Plains Zebra (Burchell's Zebra)
(Pitse e Tilodi)
Equus burchellii (**1,36 m H**)
Most common of the 3 zebra species in
southern Africa; black and white stripes have
brown shadow lines; no zebra has same
pattern; stripes serve as camouflage, with the
herd appearing as one unit, which creates
confusion for predators; highly
dependent on water; formidable
fighters, using teeth
and hooves.

Blue Wildebeest ▼
(Kgokong e pududu)
Connochaetes taurinus (**1,5 m H**)
Gregarious; territorial males rub facial glands on
tree trunks or mark territory on the ground;
short-grass grazers, therefore often seen with
zebra, impala and giraffe which eat the taller
grasses; they also rely on
other animals' eye-sight
and alertness;
pregnant female
separates herself
from herd to give
birth; calves,
mobile within
minutes of birth, are
ready to join the
herd within
1 - 2 days.

OTHER MAMMALS

Out in the bush it's all about finding enough food to eat, but also avoiding being eaten. These animals prefer the rich fruits, tubers and seeds, but they also form an important part of many predator diets.

All these animals, except the Slender Mongoose, live in social groups because the benefits they gain from this increase their chances of survival. One of the benefits is greater protection from predators.

Monkeys and baboons have sentinels keeping watch for predators. Someone in the warthog family will be looking up while the others are foraging heads to the ground.

▲ **Rock Dassie** (Pela)
Procavia capensis (**54 cm L**)
Herbivorous, spending early morning or late afternoon feeding at a furious rate; regularly bask in the sun to increase body temperature; eyesight and hearing acute; very agile with glandular secretions on soles of feet to prevent slipping; it is claimed that they have different alarm calls for eagles, leopards and pythons.

▼ **Warthog** (Kolobe ya Naga)
Phacochoerus aethiopicus (**70 cm H**)
Males have prominent tusks and 2 pairs of facial warts to protect eyes during fights; tusks used for digging, defence and fighting; often seen running with tails held stiffly upright; not territorial; feed by kneeling on front legs and dig out roots and rhizomes; sensitive to heat, cold and drought – mud wallowing protects against ultraviolet rays and parasites; use old antbear holes for shelter and breeding.

Bushpig (Kolobe ya naga) ►
Potamochoerus porcus (**60 - 85 cm H**)
Use their snouts to root out bulbs, but will also browse shrubs and eat insects, frogs, small mammals and even carrion; can be extremely dangerous if cornered or surprised; sows construct grass haystacks in dense cover as a place to give birth to their striped piglets; nocturnal but sometimes seen in the day.

Slender Mongoose (Tshagane) ▲
Galerella sanguinea
(**60 cm L, including tail**)
Solitary, diurnal; will take to trees
when threatened; inquisitive,
sometimes standing upright before
disappearing with flick of tail;
omnivorous; young will often follow
their mother in procession; main
enemy are large birds of prey.

Chacma Baboon (Tshwene) ▼
Papio ursinus (**1,5 m L**)
Largest primate in southern Africa; biggest enemy is the
leopard; eats plants, insects, scorpions, fruit, rodents, eggs
and even small mammals; highly gregarious, occurring in
troops of up to 100 with strict order of dominance;
females in season have large crimson backsides and only
mate with dominant males; senior males act as sentries
and warn other animals of predators.

▼**Vervet Monkey** (Kgabo)
Cercopithecus aethiops (**1,4 m L**)
Totem animal of the Bakgatla
tribe; sociable animals which
groom each other to remove pests
and strengthen bonds; adult male
has blue scrotum; prefer fruit and
pods, but also eat insects, eggs and
small birds; main enemies are
leopards and eagles.

Tree Squirrel (Setlhora) ▼
Paraxerus cepapi
(**35 cm L, including tail**)
Nest in old barbet or woodpecker
nests; feed on ground during the day;
female produces 2 young, which
remain in tree-hole until able to
climb up and down; eat fruit, nuts
and sometimes insects; enemies are
birds of prey, genets and pythons;
when meeting a snake they mob it
hysterically.

NOCTURNAL MAMMALS

Nocturnal mammals have several adaptations such as enlarged eyes and ears or an acute sense of smell to help them survive in low-light conditions. Most of them are solitary to ensure stealthy behaviour that avoids detection, but they also have a variety of defence strategies. Bushbabies use their own scent-marked trail as a guide to scamper back to safety – at considerable speed.

Hares lie motionless with their long ears pinned back, while pangolins roll themselves up into a ball of heavy-scaled armour. The porcupine raises its rattling coat of quills, and the aardwolf erects its mane of long hair to enlarge its appearance. The Honey Badger on the other hand, is known to defend itself aggressively and fearlessly.

▼ Aardvark (Antbear) (Thakadu)
Orycteropus afer (**1,6 m L, including tail**)
Strong bear-like claws dig for ants and termites, then uses 30 cm, sticky tongue; excavated termite mounds become burrows for many other animals like hyaena, warthog and even bats and owls; solitary, has very poor eyesight but keen senses of smell and hearing; has scent glands between back legs.

▼ Smith's Red Rock Rabbit (Mmutla)
Pronolagus rupestris (**45 cm L**)
Common, solitary, reddish-brown rabbits with distinctive rusty-brown legs, rump and tail; occur in boulder-strewn areas, grasslands and scrub at all altitudes; hide in rock crevices during the day; piles of pale brown droppings in latrines between the rocks give their presence away.

Scrub Hare (Mmutla) ▼
Lepus saxatilis (**55 cm L**)
Can often be seen darting ahead of cars at night; a grazer that eats its own dung pellets to obtain full nutrients; males fight viciously over females; unlike rabbits, baby hares can run soon after birth; their defence is to lie still with ears flattened; they also swim well; preyed on by many carnivores and large birds of prey.

Large-spotted Genet (Nakedi/Tshipa) ▼
Genetta tigrina (**1 m L, including tail**)
Black-tipped tail distinguishes it from Small-spotted Genet; each one has own unique body pattern; stalk prey in leopard fashion, catching insects, spiders, birds, reptiles and small rodents.

▲ Aardwolf (Mmabudu/Mabudu)
Proteles cristatus (**50 cm H**)
Long mane often raised in excitement; long curved canines, but other teeth reduced in size; eats up to 200 000 insects a night, mainly termites.

▼ Lesser Bushbaby (Kgajwanamasigo)
Galago moholi
(37 cm L, including tail)
Live in trees; forage alone for gum and insects but sleep in
family groups in a platform nest with tail and hands covering
huge eyes; wipe urine on their feet to scent-mark; make sounds
like a baby crying; preyed on by genets and owls.

▼ African Civet (Tsaparangaka)
Civettictis civetta **(40 cm H)**
Claws are doglike and non-retractable; territorial
and solitary; dung contains seed, hair
and exoskeletons of millipedes;
secretion from anal glands
was once used in
perfumes.

▼ Pangolin (Kgaga)
Manis temminckii **(1,1 m L)**
Eat mainly ants; use their large front claws to tear
open termite mounds; forage close to the surface
or under decomposing plant matter; roll into a
ball when alarmed to protect their soft
underparts; have been hunted almost to extinction
for their supposed
medicinal qualities.

Porcupine (Noko) ▲
Hystrix africaeaustralis **(85 cm L)**
Largest rodent in Africa; will walk backwards
towards an intruder with vibrating quills raised,
sometimes inflicting fatal wounds; can travel 20
km a night foraging for tubers, bulbs or roots;
ring-barks trees and gnaws bones to sharpen
incisors and obtain minerals.

▼ Honey Badger (Magogwe)
Mellivora capensis **(95 cm L)**
Tough and aggressive animals that will eat almost
anything, including carrion, fruit, small
mammals and birds, honey and bee larvae;
usually only seen at night; sometimes
found scavenging around camps for
discarded food.

23

REPTILES AND AMPHIBIANS

Once you get beyond the misconception that reptiles and amphibians are cold, slimy and dangerous, you will discover the fascinating world of these creatures. Like other animals, they too show distinct habitat preferences, and their diversity matches those of birds and other animals.

Species details:
• Length is measured in millimetres, centimetres or metres

REPTILES

Crocodiles, Water Monitors and Marsh Terrapins are all found near or in water. Terrapins are often amusing to watch as they balance on rocks or logs over water basking in the sun. Like all reptiles, they are using the sun to raise their body temperature, as they cannot do it themselves.

The rest are not associated with water, and may be terrestrial (living on the ground) or arboreal (living above the ground). Skinks, geckos and agamas fall into the latter category, but are also found on rocky outcrops where they escape predators. Tortoises are in the former category, constrained by the hard, heavy shell on their backs that serves as protection.

Common Striped Skink (Sefeleko) ▲
Mabuya striata (18 - 20 cm)
Common in a variety of habitats; forage for small invertebrates on rocky outcrops and in trees and houses; they are the prey of jackals and many other predators.

◄ **Moreau's Tropical House Gecko** (Sepharela-Nkong)
Hemidactylus mabouia mabouia (12 - 15 cm)
Lives under tree bark; may be seen actively hunting insects on the walls and roofs of homes at night; males vigorously defend their territories, chasing or fighting off other males.

◄ **Rock Monitor** (Gopane)
Varanus exanthematicus albigularis (0,7 - 1,3 m)
Huge lizard, related to the Komodo Dragon; feeds on tortoises, eggs, insects, small birds, rodents and carrion; lives in tunnels under rock overhangs or disused animal burrows or termite mounds; it is a protected animal. An old Tswana story says that this lizard, Gopane, sucks milk from the goat by winding its tail around the goat's legs and then milking it.

Nile Crocodile (Kwena) ▼
Crocodylus niloticus (2,5-3,5 m; max 5,9 m)
Oldest surviving animal on earth; inbuilt barometer detects changes in atmospheric pressure; 50 - 70 eggs laid in hole in sand; eggs on top become males due to greater heat; mother carries young in mouth to water, after which they are independent; prey on antelope, fish and any unsuspecting animal at water's edge; they cannot chew.

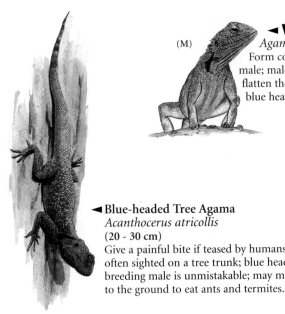

(M)

◄▼ Southern Rock Agama (Rankgatakwane)
Agama atra (20 - 25 cm; max 32 cm)
Form colonies with several females and a dominant
male; male often seen doing press-ups to intimidate rivals;
flatten their bodies when in danger, and the male's bright
blue head-colour fades to blend with surrounding rocks.

(F)

◄Blue-headed Tree Agama
Acanthocerus atricollis
(20 - 30 cm)
Give a painful bite if teased by humans;
often sighted on a tree trunk; blue head of
breeding male is unmistakable; may move
to the ground to eat ants and termites.

Water Monitor (Polometsing) ▼
Varanus niloticus
(1 - 1,4 m; max 2 m)
Largest lizards in Africa; good swimmers; found
alongside rivers and pans where they hunt a
variety of aquatic fauna; adept at locating and
raiding nests of terrapins, crocodiles and sea
turtles, as well as birds' nests; preyed upon in turn
by crocodiles, pythons and the larger eagles.

Helmeted Marsh Terrapin (Rantlapere)▼
Pelomedusa subrufa (28 cm)
Opportunistic feeders that are known to
remove ticks from wallowing animals;
sometimes hunt birds from a submerged
position; when pans are dry, bury
themselves in the mud and
hibernate until the
rains come, or
move overland
to other waters.

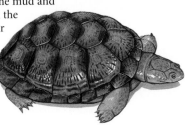

Leopard Tortoise (Khudu) ▼
Geochelone pardalis babcocki
(30 - 40 cm; max 72 cm)
Widely distributed in South Africa; most active
during or just after the rains; hibernate during cold
winter months; eat plants
and fruit; hatchlings
vulnerable to
predation by
carnivorous
animals
and birds.

Reptiles and Amphibians (continued)

Snakes have survived against difficult physical odds: they are limbless, have simple teeth, need to swallow prey whole and are relatively slow. Like the Southern African Python, many perfected the technique of constriction – tightly coiling their body around live prey to suffocate it.

Others, like the boomslang, adders, cobra and mamba, developed venom glands. Although this venom could be used for defence, most take several hours to take effect, allowing the attacker time to then kill the snake. Snakes therefore, rather deter attack by giving conspicuous warning displays. The most dramatic is the rearing cobra. To avoid being trod upon, well-camouflaged snakes like the puffadder, will give a noisy, hissing warning (while puffing itself up).

AMPHIBIANS

Frogs and toads are essentially water-dependent. Most need moist habitats for breeding and early stages of life. Rain frogs, amazingly, have evolved to survive every stage of development on land.

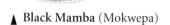

▲ **Black Mamba** (Mokwepa)
Dendroaspis polylepis (2,5 - 4,2 m)
Can be found sun-bathing on rocks, or travelling swiftly through the grass with coffin-shaped head held high; will readily attack if threatened; neurotoxic venom causes paralysis of victim's lungs with death in hours if not treated with anti-venom; preys on dassies, game-birds, rodents and lizards.

▲ **Spotted Bush Snake** (Legwere)
Philothamnus semivariegatus
(70 - 100 cm; max 126 cm)
Has a flat-bottomed belly with flat sides, green body with black spots on its front, golden brown towards the tail; a very good climber; eats lizards and small reptiles; quick to bite but the bite is harmless.

◀ **Puff Adder** (Lebolobolo)
Bitis arietans arietans
(60 - 100 cm)
Exceptionally well camouflaged; slow to move away when threatened, striking with lightning speed when startled or stepped on; potent cytotoxin causes extensive swelling and tissue death – if untreated the victim could lose a limb or die; prey mainly on rodents.

Boomslang ▲
Dispholidus typus
(1,2 - 1,6 m)
Large "tree snake" (boomslang in Afrikaans); distinctive big eyes; colour varies from mottled grey in juveniles, to brown in females, and various shades of green in males; hunt during the day; eat mainly chameleons and birds, often raiding birds' nests; very venomous, but so shy that humans are seldom bitten.

◀ **Mozambique Spitting Cobra**
Naja mossambica (1,0 - 1,3 m)
Extremely dangerous when disturbed; easily recognisable as they raise the front part of their bodies off the ground and expand their necks to form the characteristic "hood"; eject venom as far as two metres through two hollow fangs to accurately hit the enemy's eyes; don't need to raise themselves, so can spit from beneath a log or rock.

◄ Southern African Python (Tlhware)
Python natalensis **(3 - 5 m)**
Usually hunts at night, detecting warm-blooded prey with heat sensors on its lips; bite is non-venomous, with prey killed by suffocation, e.g. birds, reptiles, small mammals, including antelope and monkeys; protected species but vulnerable as skins used in the fashion industry.

▲ Red Toad (Segwagwa)
Bufo carens **(7 cm)**
Abundant towards end of summer; travel far in search of a dark, quiet place to spend the winter – shoes left in cupboards often serve this purpose well!

**Banded Rubber Frog ▼
(Gomlastiekpadda)**
Phrynomantis bifasciatus
(5 cm)
Walk and waddle, rather than jump; dig holes backwards for hibernation; lay about 600 eggs in a mass of soft jelly, attached to surface vegetation of pans and swamps.

▼ Grey Tree Frog (Foam-nest Frog)
Chiromantis xerampelina
(7 - 8 cm)
The foam is sperm that other males have paddled to froth; this holds the eggs before hatching.

▼ Rain Frog (Blaasop)
Breviceps adsperus
(7 cm)
Walk and waddle, rather than jump; dig holes backwards for hibernation; cannot swim; appear for three months after the first rains to mate; jelly-encapsulated eggs laid in holes in the ground.

Bull Frog (Reuse Brulpadda)
Pyxicephalus adspersus
(Diameter: up to 20 cm)
Have powerful hind legs; swim and jump very well; found in shallow ponds and in recently flooded grasslands.

Striped Stream Frog ▼
(Segwagwa)
Rana fasciata **(3,5 cm)**
Found in water bodies that have grassy banks; due to striped colour pattern they are well camouflaged in the long grass.

27

BIRDLIFE

Pilanesberg has over 300 bird species to share with the bird enthusiast. Each has adapted to the different habitats that Pilanesberg offers. To survive in their environment, they have developed unique methods of feeding, flight, mating and protecting themselves and their brood. Watch with wonder.

Species details:
- Length is measured in centimetres from beak-tip to tail-tip, or beak-tip to toe-tip (whichever is longer).
- Roberts bird numbers are given in brackets.
- The Tswana names of the species, where possible, have been written in brackets.

BIRDS IN HILLSIDE AND ROCKY AREAS

On the left are birds predominantly viewed on vegetated hillsides. The Crested Barbet and the larks can be seen perched conspicuously, while the Southern Pied Babblers fly from bush to bush.

On the right are birds that inhabit rocky areas. They utilise this land formation to create naturally protected nurseries. The Rock Martin builds a cup-shaped mud home against a vertical rock wall, and the Red-winged Starling a mud bowl bound with plant fibres, on rocky ledges. The Mocking Chat makes the Lesser-striped Swallow's mud pellet bowl its home, sometimes ousting the original builder. The Verreaux's Eagle creates a large stick platform; while another raptor, the Common Kestrel simply lays its clutch of eggs on a rocky cliff ledge.

Look out for white streaks of bird droppings on the cliff face and follow them upwards. You may be rewarded with the joy of sighting the home of a nesting pair.

◀ **Crested Barbet** (Kokopa)
Trachyphonus vaillantii
(**23 cm**) (**473**)
Common, colourful bird; perches conspicuously; gives call like an alarm clock lasting about 30 seconds; hops around on the ground with tail and crest erect; bores nesting holes in soft-wood tree trunks, raising up to four broods (Aug – Feb).

▼ **Southern Pied Babbler**
Turdoides bicolor (**26 cm**) (**563**)
Entirely white except for black wings and tail; immature birds are initially olive-brown; often found in thornveld; moves in noisy groups, calling a high-pitched '*kwee kwee kwee kweer*'; forages on ground for insects.

◀ **Sabota Lark** (Sebota)
Mirafra sabota (**15 cm**) (**498**)
Mimics about 60 other species; usually solitary; forages on open ground for insects and seeds; not known to drink water.

Rufous-naped Lark ▶
Mirafra africana (**18 cm**) (**494**)
Usually seen perched conspicuously, uttering a '*tsee oo*' sound, and rattling wings; dipping flight stops abruptly when it drops into grass and runs in crouched fashion, looking for seeds and insects; also found in grasslands.

▼ Common Kestrel (Rock Kestrel) ►
Falco tinnunculus **(32 cm) (181)**
Can often be seen hovering, then taking prey
from the ground; do not build nests, but lay
their eggs on ledges, in holes, trees or old nests
of other birds; feed on small mammals,
lizards, snakes, insects and other birds.

Mocking Chat ►
Thamnolaea cinnamomeiventris
(22 cm) (593)
Vocal birds with a loud melodious song which mimics
about 30 other bird calls; occur in small groups;
can be seen running around, sometimes raising
tails; drop onto insects on the ground from perch,
or jump around in trees in search of fruit.

(M)   (F)

◄ Red-winged Starling
(Legodi)
Onychognathus morio
(28 cm) (769)
Slender, elegant, glossy
black with chestnut
wingtips; often found in
large flocks of 100 or
more; has a varied diet
of fruit, insects,
reptiles, ticks and
aloe nectar.

▲ Rock Martin ►
(Peolwane)
Hirundo fuligula
(15 cm) (529)
Small brown swallow with
square white spotted tail;
often flies around with other
swallows feeding on insects;
perches on rocks; builds neat
cup-like nest of mud against
vertical cliffs.

Verreaux's Eagle (Black Eagle) (Ntsu) ►
Aquila verreauxii **(84 cm) (131)**
Uncommon, large eagle, totally black, with a white
'V' on the back and rump; yellow feet and cere; live
in pairs, forming permanent bonds; nest in winter
against sheer cliff faces, utilising the same nest for
generations; female lays 2 eggs a few days apart;
the older chick kills the younger one; feed
mainly on dassies, but also other mammals,
terrestrial birds, carrion and rarely
reptiles; can sometimes be seen in flight
or perched on rocks.

29

Birds in Grasslands and Sand Roads

Grasslands are mainly found at high altitude in southern Africa. Illustrated here, the francolins and korhaans (page 32) are the most characteristic birdlife of this habitat.

Sand roads, though not a natural habitat, attract certain animals. For seed-eating birds, like francolins, food is easier to find along the grassy road edge. Birds of prey scan for easy pickings on the open area. As you travel, watch for the soaring Black-chested Snake Eagle and the hovering Black-shouldered Kite. Manouvering above the grasslands are the Lilac-breasted Roller and Pin-tailed Whydah, who in breeding season put on wonderful flight displays.

Not all birds however are keen to exhibit their flying abilities. Although their flight is strong over short distances, the naturally shy and wary francolins, prefer to crouch in dense cover when disturbed.

Black-shouldered Kite ▼ ►
Elanus caeruleus
(30 cm) (127)
Can often be seen perched at the roadside flicking its tail up repeatedly, or hovering 100 m above ground and swooping down on rodents, insects, lizards and birds; prey is carried in the feet and eaten while perched.

Lilac-breasted Roller (Letlekere) **▼**
Coracias caudata **(36 cm) (447)**
Remarkable colours are unmistakeable; courtship displays are spectacular tumbling aerobatics; hunting from a perch, they seize prey on the ground such as a grasshopper, sometimes eating it in flight; feed mainly on insects and small vertebrates like lizards; there is a saying the if "letlekere" perches on your house or tree it will cause bad luck, lightning and fire!

◄**Black-chested Snake Eagle** (Ntsu)
Circaetus pectoralis **(68 cm) (143)**
Can be confused with the Martial Eagle, but is smaller and in flight has white undersides with dark stripes on wings and tail; bare black and yellow legs; hovers and swoops down when a snake is sighted, kills it and eats it in flight.

Pin-tailed Whydah (Molope)
Vidua macroura
(M 34 cm; F 12 cm) (860)
Males are conspicuous, active and aggressive in
summer, spending the day chasing other birds; keep
about 6 females in breeding season; do not build
nests but lay eggs in nests of waxbills and other
small birds, relying on the hosts to rear chicks.

Natal Francolin (Lesogo) ►
Pternistes natalensis
(38 cm) (196)
Strident crowing often heard at
dusk and dawn; small flocks of
up to 10 birds; roosts in trees;
eats roots, bulbs, fruit and seeds.

Crested Francolin (Lesogo) ►
Francolinus sephaena
(33 cm) (189)
Recognisable by dark cap; noisy
at dawn and dusk; tail often
cocked like that of a bantam
chicken; pairs or small groups.

Francolins (Masogo)
Family Phasianidae
Chicken-like birds with short
tails; different species can be
identified by patterns on
undersides and by distinctive
calls; males have spurs on
back of legs; fly fast over short
distances with whirring wings.

Coqui Francolin ▼
(Lesogo)
Peliperdix coqui
(28 cm) (188)
Small species; often walks
slowly and in a stooped
fashion, especially when
out in the open; if
alarmed, will
keep still.

◄ **Swainson's Spurfowl**
(Swainson's Francolin)
(Lesogo)
Pternistes swainsonii
(38 cm) (199)
Identified by red face and
throat, and brown legs;
solitary or small
groups; males often
call from low
branches or
anthills.

BIRDS IN GRASSLANDS AND SAND ROADS (CONTINUED)

Stop and listen to the magical communication of bird song. Most birds have distinct calls which declare their territory, attract a mate or intimidate rivals. The Red-crested Korhaan, which is loud and conspicuous, is often vocal on moonlit nights; joining the nocturnal Fiery-necked Nightjar whose littany is also heard at dawn and dusk. Another call at dawn is the highly vocal Hadeda Ibis, on leaving their roost. Listen too for the loud piping song of the Golden-breasted Bunting.

Another way of seeking out birds is by their association with other creatures. An obvious example is the Cattle Egret which follows large grazing mammals, hunting for disturbed insects. The Little Bee-eater utilises termite mounds or aardvark burrows to build its nest. Also using termite mounds, or any natural hole in the ground or tree, for its home is the African Hoopoe.

▼ **African Hoopoe** (Pupupu)
Upupa epops (**26 cm**) (**451**)
Walks about probing the ground for insects; will sometimes extract insects from the bark of trees; flies in a butterfly fashion; its call is a monotonous '*hoo poop poop*'; smelly nest as they do not remove faeces; traditionally believed to bring good luck.

Little Bee-eater (Morokapula) ►
Merops pusillus (**17 cm**) (**444**)
Solitary nests in a termite mound or sandbank.

White-fronted Bee-eater ►
(Morokapula)
Merops bullockoides (**23 cm**) (**443**)
Nest colonially in 1-metre-long burrows along riverbanks.

Bee-eaters (Merokapula)
Family Meropidae
Feed on insects, especially butterflies, in the air, or they hawk from a perch, usually returning to same perch to eat prey.

Southern Black Korhaan ►
(Black Korhaan) (Tlatlagwe)
Eupodotis afra (**53 cm**) (**239**)
Males very noisy, females shy; 1 - 2 eggs laid on ground Oct – Feb.

◄ **Red-crested Korhaan**
(Tlatlagwe)
Eupodotis ruficrista
(**50 cm**) (**237**)
Very fast fliers; red crest of male seldom seen; males have acrobatic courtship flight; when threatened stand still, using camouflage to hide in the bush.

Buntings Family Fringillidae
Small, sparrow-like birds that forage on the ground beneath bushes and trees for insects and seeds.

Rock Bunting ▶
Emberiza tahapisi
(14 cm) (886)
Not as vocal as other buntings, producing a soft '*pee-wee*' call.

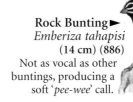

Golden-breasted Bunting ▲
Emberiza flaviventris
(16 cm) (884)
Sings frequently from a perch, call sounding like '*pretty boy*'; nest is a cup of grass stems and roots, normally in fork of tree.

Cattle Egret ▶
(Modisa dikgomo)
Bubulcus ibis
(54 cm) (71)
Acquire red bill with buff plumes on head, back and breast in breeding season; associate with large mammals in open grassy areas, feeding on insects disturbed during grazing; roost near water in the evenings, often flying in 'V' formation.

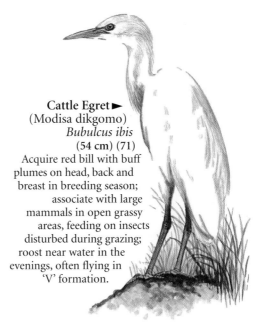

Fiery-necked Nightjar ▲
(Bomamauwane)
Caprimulgus pectoralis
(23 - 28 cm) (404 - 408)
Well-camouflaged birds with long, pointed wings; fly silently as they hawk insects, especially beetles; roost and nest on the ground moving their eggs when they suspect detection; call is an initial rising whistle of '*good lord*', ending in a series of falling trills '*deliver us*'.

Hadeda Ibis ▶
Bostrychia hagedash (76 cm) (94)
Noisy bird uttering a loud '*haaa*' on take-off and characteristic '*ha ha ha di da*' in flight; small flocks roost in trees and forage on ground, probing their bills deep into the soil for insects; also eat spiders, reptiles, crustaceans, earthworms.

Birds in Thickets

The dense growth of the thicket areas provide protection and food for a wide variety of birds. As with other animals, birds are specially adapted to specific food niches. Some birds, like the Chinspot Batis and mousebirds, clamber about the branches gleaning insects and spiders, or feeding on fruit. The Marico Flycatcher, White-browed Scrub-Robin and Dark-capped Bulbul forage on the ground.

Some of these species are associated specifically with thorn trees: the Grey Go-away-bird and Chinspot Batis nest among the thorns, no doubt for protection, whereas the Fiscal Shrike is famed for hanging its prey from the trees' spiny armour.

◄ **Arrow-marked Babbler**
(Letsheganoga)
Turdoides jardineii
(24 cm) (560)
Move around from tree to tree in noisy groups of about 10; feed mainly on insects, also spiders, small reptiles and fruit; about 7 birds help to build nest.

Marico Flycatcher ▼
Bradornis mariquensis (18 cm) (695)
Perches conspicuously on leafless outer branches of thorn trees, uttering harsh unmusical sound; catches insects on the ground; nest is a shallow bowl of roots and coarse twigs made on a horizontal branch.

◄**Black-headed Oriole**
Oriolus larvatus (25 cm) (545)
Utters beautiful, liquid call from tops of tall trees; mainly insectivorous, but will feed on fruit and nectar; it makes a deep well-concealed, moss nest, lined with spider webs and plant material.

▼ **White-browed Scrub-Robin**
(White-breasted Robin)
Erythropygia leucophrys
(15 cm) (613)
Usually seen singly or in pairs on ground or in scattered scrub; make varied, clear calls from tree-tops; 2 - 3 eggs laid on ground Oct – Dec.

◄**Common Fiscal Shrike**
(Tlhomedi)
Lanius collaris (23 cm) (732)
Hunt from perches carrying prey in beaks or feet; sometimes hang prey on thornbushes or fences, returning later to feed, hence the name 'butcher bird'.

(F) ◄**Chinspot Batis**
Batis molitor (13 cm) (701)
Often hang upside down to remove insects and spiders from leaves; call consists of 3 descending syllables, sounding like '*three blind mice*'.

(M)

Grey Go-away-bird▶
(Grey Lourie) (Mokoe)
Corythaixoides concolor **(48 cm) (373)**
The '*go away*' call alerts game when
predators approach; perch at tops of
trees and fly in laboured fashion;
roost in groups at night; usually
nest in thorn trees; eat fruit,
flowers, buds, leaves, insects
and sometimes
small birds.

White-backed Mousebird ▲
(Letsiababa)
Colius colius **(33 cm) (425)**
Occur in drier areas; sometimes
forage on ground.

Fork-tailed Drongo (Kuamesi)▶
Dicrurus adsimilis **(25 cm) (541)**
Immature birds have white wing-
patches, flashed in flight, but adults
are totally black; perch at tops of trees; are
aggressive, often harassing birds of prey; mimic
other birds but main call is a rasping squeak; catch
insects in the air, mob other birds, and also eat
small birds and sometimes fish.

◀ **Speckled Mousebird** (Letsiababa)
Colius striatus **(32 cm) (424)**
Fruit-eating birds; hang in a vertical
position in trees or scramble about
in mouse-like fashion; occur in
small flocks in dense, moist areas.

Dark-capped Bulbul ▶
(Black-eyed Bulbul)
(Rankolokota)
Pycnonotus barbatus **(22 cm) (568)**
Abundant and common in variety of
habitats; gregarious, cheerful, vocal and
active; eat insects, fruit and nectar; call
sounds like, '*Wake up Gregory*'.

BIRDS IN THICKETS (CONTINUED)

These birds are predominantly seed- and/or insect-eaters, spending much of their time foraging on the ground. Here they benefit from the shorter grass that exposes seeds and insects. Most of the birds are conspicuous and easily spotted.

As striking as the secretive Crimson-breasted Shrike is, it is more often heard than seen. Other characteristic bird calls can also be heard across the savannah; and the Cape Turtle-Dove's distinct rhythmic call often continues throughout the night along with the piping, nocturnal Spotted Thick-knee.

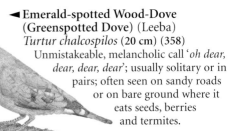

▲ **Rock Pigeon** (Leebarope) ►
Columba guinea (33 cm) (349)
Nest on cliffs; fly in flocks covering great distances to find water or food; call is a loud cooing '*doo, doo, doo, doo*' rising to a crescendo, then falling.

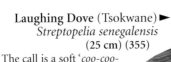

Laughing Dove (Tsokwane) ►
Streptopelia senegalensis
(25 cm) (355)
The call is a soft '*coo-coo-CUK-coo-coo*'.
Unlike Cape Turtle Dove, has no black collar; very common resident.

Doves (Maeba) Family Columbidae
Predominantly grey with small heads and stout bodies; fly extremely well but spend much time on the ground picking up seeds which are stored in well developed crops; song is typical coo-ing sound.

◄ **Emerald-spotted Wood-Dove (Greenspotted Dove)** (Leeba)
Turtur chalcospilos (20 cm) (358)
Unmistakeable, melancholic call '*oh dear, dear, dear, dear*'; usually solitary or in pairs; often seen on sandy roads or on bare ground where it eats seeds, berries and termites.

▲ **Cape Turtle-Dove** (Leeba)
Streptopelia capicola
(28 cm) (354)
Call is a harsh '*work-harder, work harder*' much repeated; has a thin, black collar round the back of the neck; males display by flapping straight upward, then coo-ing while spiralling back down to perch.

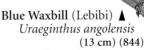

Blue Waxbill (Lebibi) ▲
Uraeginthus angolensis
(13 cm) (844)
Forage for seed on the ground; drink water regularly; nests sometimes built near wasps for protection; Pin-tailed Whydahs lay their eggs in these nests; feed in small flocks (up to 40), and fly rapidly into dense bush if alarmed.

◄**Crimson-breasted Shrike** (Mampa tshibidu)
Laniarius atrococcineus (**25 cm**) (**739**)
Associated with dry, semi-arid thornveld; vocal
birds, seen alone or in pairs, foraging on ground
for insects; called '*Reichsvogel*' in Namibia as colours
are same as German flag; the birds call in a duet
almost simultaneously '*qui-quip-chiri*'.

▼ **Red-billed Firefinch**
Lagonosticta senegala (**10 cm**) (**842**)
A remarkable red bird, with a pink
bill; flies to nearest cover when
disturbed; occurs in pairs or
small parties.

Jameson's Firefinch ▼
Lagonosticta rhodopareta
(**11 cm**) (**841**)
The reddest
of all the
firefinches;
bill blackish;
occurs in bushveld.

Firefinches Family Estrildidae
Gregarious; feed on ground for
seed, often at water; host to
Widowfinches, incubating and
rearing their young.

Spotted Thick-knee ►
(**Spotted Dikkop**) (**Mmutlanakana**)
Burhinus capensis (**44 cm**) (**297**)
Insectivorous; can be seen sleeping during the day in
shade; run with head low when disturbed; calls a piping
'*ti ti ti ti tee*' rising in pitch and volume, then dying down.

◄**Helmeted Guineafowl** (Kgaka)
Numida meleagris (**58 cm**) (**203**)
Roost in trees at night; congregate in large
flocks on the ground where they forage for
seeds, bulbs and insects; have been seen
removing ticks from warthogs; they are
among our best-loved and noisiest birds
with their much repeated '*ker-bek-ker-bek-
ker-bek, krrrr*'.

Birds in Thickets (continued)

Thickets provide nesting opportunities for many birds. While the Cardinal Woodpecker and Black-collared Barbet tunnel their own holes in dead trees, other birds like the Spotted Eagle-Owl utilise cavities that nature provides. The Green Wood-Hoopoe and Pearl-spotted Owlet usually use woodpecker- or barbet-excavated holes. The vulnerable female hornbill, who has shed her feathers to incubate the nest, is sealed in a tree trunk hole, while the male feeds her through a small beak-slit.

The Spotted Eagle-Owl uses holes in trees but also favours old raptor nests or even creates a nest on top of a Hamerkop nest!

Green Wood-Hoopoe► (Redbilled Woodhoopoe)
Phoeniculus purpureus (36 cm) (452)
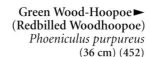

Occur in noisy, restless groups which move from tree to tree, clambering around branches looking for insects, millipedes and small reptiles; they nest in holes made by woodpeckers and barbets.

◄Cardinal Woodpecker
(Kokopa) *Dendropicos fuscescens* (15 cm) (486)
Often heard making rapid tapping noises on branches; usually work a tree from bottom up to the top, looking for grubs and insects; excavate holes in dead trees for nesting.

◄Spotted Eagle-Owl (Morubitshi) ▼
Bubo africanus (47 cm) (401)

Most common owl in southern Africa; has slit ears behind the eyes; hunts rodents, small mammals, reptiles and birds; lays eggs under rocky overhangs, in hollow tree-stumps, or in other birds' nests; call is a typical hooting 'hu hoo'; it is traditionally associated with bad luck as it can 'invite' witches to your house; it is also said about owls, '*Morubitshi ga o bonwe, o bonwe ke Motsoga pele*', which means 'only early risers see unusual things'.

Pearl-spotted Owlet (Morubitshi) ▼
Glaucidium perlatum (18 cm) (398)
Smallest owl in southern Africa weighing 50 gm; has false eyes on back of head; active at dawn and dusk; often mobbed by other birds when resting; hunts insects, birds and bats; call is a repetitive ascending '*tee tee tee tee teeu teeu teeu*' then descending.

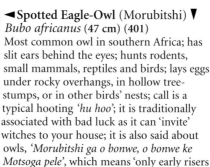

Black-collared Barbet (Kokopa) ▼
Lybius torquatus (20 cm) (464)
Sexes alike; usually in pairs but also in larger groups making raucous noise, especially in summer during breeding; eat fruit (especially figs) and insects; also found in riverine areas.

Kingfishers
Both nest in holes – the Brown-hooded in a one-metre-long tunnel in earth banks, the Striped in a hole in a tree; species vary greatly in size; in spite of their names, neither of these species eat fish – their diet consists of insects and small lizards.

Brown-hooded Kingfisher ►
Halcyon albiventris
(24 cm) (435)
Common and noisy; solitary or
in pairs with an open-winged,
bobbing display; deep red bill
with blackish tip.

◄ Striped Kingfisher
Halcyon chelicuti
(18 cm) (437)
Smaller than Brown-hooded Kingfisher,
with white collar and a lower red and
upper black bill; solitary or in pairs.

Red-billed Hornbill (Korwe) ►
Tockus erythrorhynchus **(46 cm) (458)**
Black and white mottled upperparts and a
distinctive red bill; forages on ground; eats
insects, seed scorpions and amphibians.

Hornbills (Dikorwe) Family Bucerotidae
Nesting behaviour of both hornbills is similar – both nest in holes in tree trunks, with the female sealed inside with only a slit for her beak to protrude, and for the male to pass food through; after 20 days, female breaks out, the chicks reseal the nest and are fed by both parents; ungainly looping flight.

◄ Southern Yellow-billed Hornbill (Korwe)
Tockus leucomelas **(55 cm) (459)**
Large, distinctive yellow bill; often in
campsites; eats from fruiting trees
and the ground.

Cape Glossy Starling (Legodi) ►
Lamprotornis nitens **(24 cm) (764)**
Small flocks; pair off in breeding season; distinctive high-
pitched croaking *'turr treau'* call; feed on insects, fruit and
aloe nectar; fond of camp titbits; they can be a delight,
performing aerobatics before roosting at night. There is a
Tswana story about children and this starling "Legodi" … if a
spoilt child wants this bird, you must give it to him, because
the bird will peck the child and teach it a lesson.

WATERBIRDS

Generally waterbirds swim or dive using webbed or lobed feet, or are long-legged which means they can forage in relatively deep water. Long legs also means their eyes are at a higher vantage point to detect prey from a greater distance.

Some eat fish, while most eat invertebrates off the water surface, or bottom sediments and aquatic vegetation. Plovers, with their shorter legs, prefer open ground along the water's edge where they probe the mud for food. The long-toed Black Crake and African Jacana wander over floating plants, pecking at the surface or turning leaves for a nourishing find.

◄ **White-throated Swallow**
(Peolwane)
Hirundo albigularis
(17 cm) (520)
Inter-African migrant; seen alone or in pairs, near water, catching insects in air; will often perch on stumps and posts in water.

Three-banded Plover ▼
Charadrius tricollaris (18 cm) (249)
Fearless bird, venturing among the feet of elephants and buffalo at water's edge; utters a high-pitched '*wheet*' while running around, suddenly stopping to prod the mud for insects and worms; nest is a mere scraping near the waterline with a few stones added; 1-3 well-camouflaged eggs laid.

Blacksmith Lapwing ►
(Blacksmith Plover)
(Lethullatshipi)
Vanellus armatus (30 cm) 258
Found in pairs or small groups; eat and nest on the shorelines of water bodies; extremely vocal, 'screeching' when their nest is threatened; nest simply an exposed scrape in the soil, but eggs are well camouflaged.

Lesser Masked Weaver (Thaga) ▼
Ploceus intermedius
(15 cm) (815)
Males have black masks in breeding season; weave rounded nests with grass ends sticking out and vertical tunnel-entrance; nests often hang over water; man-made dams often create new habitats for these weavers; will breed in colonies of not more than 10 birds.

◄ **Egyptian Goose** (Legou)
Alopochen aegyptiacus (70 cm) (102)
Grazes on short, cropped grass and eats insects during the breeding season to boost protein intake; nests in trees or on buildings; chicks plunge from dizzy heights and head straight for water; females utter a honking sound, males wheeze; mate for life.

◄ African Jacana
Actophilornis africanus (25 - 30 cm) 240
Also known as Lily-trotters because they walk
on floating plants to move about the water
surface; hunt for insects, crustaceans and
snails; have exceptionally long toes for
balance and to spread their weight; males
look after eggs and chicks, carrying them
around under their wings, while
females find next mate of the season.

Little Grebe (Dabchick) (Sefodi) ▼
Tachybaptus ruficollis (20 cm) (8)
Sometimes rears up out of the water, flapping
wings in display; will often follow hippo, picking
up disturbed insects and tadpoles; absorbs heat in
winter by pointing tail to the sun, exposing the
black skin.

▼ Black Crake
Amaurornis flavirostra (21 cm) 213
Bright red legs and eyes, and yellow
beak make a striking contrast to the
black body; usually seen walking over
floating vegetation in reedy or marshy
areas; unusual call can be heard in
reedbeds – an explosive '*rr-rr-rr*'
ending in a croak; eat insects, snails,
crabs, worms, small fish, small birds,
herons' eggs, seeds and water plants.

◄ Spur-winged Goose (Legou)
Plectropterus gambensis
(1 m) (116)
Largest waterfowl in South Africa,
weighing up to 10 kg; large flocks in non-
breeding season; male has long spurs on
wings for fighting; eats grass shoots, tubers,
seeds and aquatic plants.

WATERBIRDS (CONTINUED)

Every waterbird has developed unique ways of hunting or foraging for their food. The Grey Heron is equipped with a long bill to grab or spear its meal. The African Darter and White-breasted Cormorant are strong underwater swimmers where they pursue their prey.

The ducks can be found sifting through mud and aquatic vegetation with their flat bills looking for invertebrates. The Hamerkop stirs up mud with its feet searching for a meal, while Fish Eagles and kingfishers perch high over the water from where they can spot their prey.

◄ **White-faced Duck** (Sefodi)
Dendrocygna viduata (**48 cm**) (**99**)
A beautifully marked bird with a very upright stance; has a musical 3-note whistle; dives and forages under-water for aquatic plants and insects; occurs in large numbers around edges of water.

▼ **Yellow-billed Duck** (Sefodi)
Anas undulata (**60 cm**) (**104**)
Diagnostic features are bright yellow bill with a central black patch; dabbles on water, upending itself to find insects and larvae; often found in pairs or flocks.

Pied Kingfisher ►
Ceryle rudis (**28 cm**) (**428**)
The only black-and-white kingfisher; usually found in pairs; hovers frequently, with long, straight bill pointing downwards, before splashing into water to catch small fish or insects; nests in holes in sandbanks.

Hamerkop (Mamasiloanoka) ▼
Scopus umbretta (**56 cm**) (**81**)
Stand in shallow water; stir mud with feet, looking for frogs and fish; build huge dome-like nest of reeds, twigs and grass (up to 50 kg); entrance made of weak material giving way under weight of intruding predators.

Grey Heron ▲
Ardea cinerea (**1 m**) (**62**)
Plain grey underwing in flight; legs and feet turn reddish in breeding season; usually solitary, stabbing at insects, fish, frogs and crabs; will sometimes feed at night; roost communally.

◄ African Fish Eagle (Kgoadira)
Haliaeetus vocifer **(73 cm) (148)**
Spend most of the day perched in trees
watching for fish which they scoop out
with their feet, in full flight; loud
distinctive call made with head thrown
back, even in flight; mate for life.

White-breasted Cormorant ▲
Phalacrocorax lucidus **(90 cm) (55)**
Largest cormorant in South Africa; flies
fast, low over water; swims partly
submerged when alarmed; catches frogs,
fish and other aquatic animals.

(M)

Giant Kingfisher ►
Megaceryle maxima **(46 cm) 429**
Largest of the kingfishers, with
speckled black-and-white backs; perch
over water, looking for fish, crabs or frogs
within range; favourite branches often
coated with fish scales; nest in tunnels
burrowed into river or stream banks.

◄ African Darter
Anhinga melanogaster **(79 cm) (60)**
Swim submerged with only snake-like
necks sticking out; pierce prey
underwater with sharp
bills, then swallow whole;
lack oil glands and often
seen drying wings in
the sun.

Large Birds

Birds have evolved to survive with the aid of flight: to migrate long distances, to enhance their feeding abilities, to attract a mate, and as a means of protection. The large birds here illustrate these aspects. Migrant birds, like the Wahlberg's Eagle, possess incredible endurance, and fly vast distances using highly advanced navigational skills. Vultures take to the air only well after sunrise, because it takes time for the ground to warm up and develop the thermals needed to support their weight. They cover a wide area in search of food.

In breeding season the Secretarybird has an impressive courtship flight. The world's heaviest flying bird, the Kori Bustard, flies only when threatened, while the world's largest bird, the Ostrich, is flightless. It seems to have survived on a continent populated by powerful predators only because of its speed and kicking abilities.

▼ **Secretarybird** (Ramolongwana)
Sagittarius serpentarius (**1,5 m**) (**118**)
Terrestrial bird of prey; loose plume-like quills look like olden day secretaries' pens; walk proudly, stopping to shuffle feet in search of insects, rodents and reptiles; snakes are circled with widespread wings, trampled to death, then swallowed whole.

◄**Kori Bustard** (Kgori)
Ardeotis kori (**1,3 m**) (**230**)
Heaviest flying bird in the world, with males weighing up to 19 kg; only fly when threatened; usually occur alone, but may congregate in flocks of 30 or more; eat seed, carrion and small vertebrates; male inflates neck and fans tail over back to attract female.

Ostrich (Ntshwe) ►
Struthio camelus (**2 m**) (**1**)
World's largest bird weighing up to 156 kg; can run up to 70 km/h; eat pebbles to assist digestion; male has a lion-like roar, often at night; male and female protect nest, sometimes giving fatal kicks to intruders.

Tawny Eagle (Ntsu) ▼
Aquila rapax (**70 cm**) (**132**)
Not common in this area but present
all year round; make large nests at
top of trees in winter; seen in pairs
or singly; varied, scruffy
plumage; recognised by
pale-yellow cere and gape
ending just below eye.

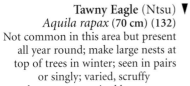

Wahlberg's Eagle (Ntsu) ►
Aquila wahlbergi
(**60 cm**) (**135**)
The only brown eagle to breed
in South Africa in summer;
also a migrant bird,
occuring singly or in pairs;
fairly common and
recognised by deep yellow
cere, gape and legs.

Lappet-faced Vulture (Lenong)►
Torgos tracheliotus (**1 m**) (**124**)
Largest resident vulture dominating
carcasses; can tear open tough skin with
massive bills; female larger than male;
known to attack live prey.

◄ **Cape Vulture**
(Lenong)
Gyps coprotheres
(**1,1 m**) (**122**)
Endemic to southern Africa; at one
time, most common vulture in South
Africa, but threatened by farmers as it has been
known to attack sheep; numbers also reducing
because of chick mortality; nests communally on
cliff ledges which become white with
their droppings.

Vultures (Manong)
Large, scavenging birds of prey that clean up
carcasses and prevent the spread of disease;
soar high on thermals, using excellent sight to
find the kills; cannot grip prey with talons, but
use powerful beaks to tear carcasses open; all
have bald or sparsely haired heads as an
adaptation to the bloody feeding conditions.

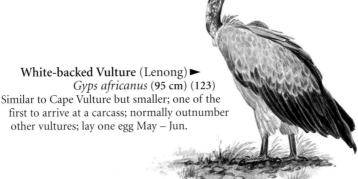

White-backed Vulture (Lenong) ►
Gyps africanus (**95 cm**) (**123**)
Similar to Cape Vulture but smaller; one of the
first to arrive at a carcass; normally outnumber
other vultures; lay one egg May – Jun.

Plants and Insects

The landscape of Pilanesberg has been created through geological processes. The resulting rolling hills, mounds of displaced rock, gulleys, hollows and valleys form the base for the plantlife that has established here. The nutrient-rich, life-sustaining soil and climate also play an important role. The vegetated habitats in turn are sources of food, shelter and safety for all animal life.

Species details:
• Height is measured in metres or centimetres
• National tree numbers are given in brackets

Hillsides

Plants growing on hillsides are affected by the slope's position with regard to the sun. North or west-facing slopes are exposed to the sun for long periods which cause the soil on these slopes to dry out. Plants that thrive under these kinds of hot, sunny conditions do not require much water. The Red Bushwillow and Live-long Lannea are characteristic. Generally south and east-facing slopes, that are only exposed to morning sunlight, are shady and cool and retain more moisture. Because it is wetter here, trees often form dense stands. Many tall-growing grasses also thrive in these conditions.

Golden Beard Grass ►
Chrysopogon serrulatus
(1 m)

▲ **Praying Mantis** (Maseletswana)
Sphodromantis gastrica (**85 mm**)
Slow-moving predatory insect; when sitting back on hind legs looks as if its praying; the front legs will shoot out to seize prey.

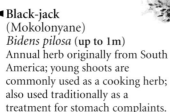

◄**Black-jack**
(Mokolonyane)
Bidens pilosa (**up to 1m**)
Annual herb originally from South America; young shoots are commonly used as a cooking herb; also used traditionally as a treatment for stomach complaints.

Nightshade ▼
Solanum species
(**up to 50 cm**)
Belongs to the Potato Family; flowers may be mauve, yellow or white, usually small, star-shaped or circular; common species include Bitter Apple, Poison Apple and Wild Tomato; spherical yellow-red fruits should all be regarded as poisonous.

Live-long Lannea ▲
(Mmotshwana/Molebatsi)
Lannea discolor (**up to 8 m**) (**362**)
Single trunked, branching into a few thick branches that spread to form a sparse irregular canopy; creamy-yellow flowers appear early April; tasty, purple-black fruit; said to cure fever and constipation; poles, fishing floats, twine and spoons are made from the soft wood.

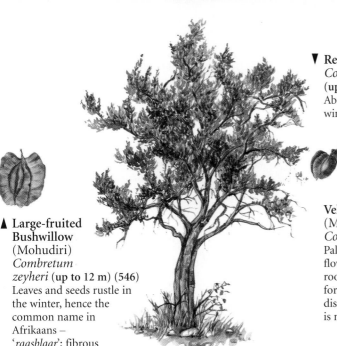

Red Bushwillow (Mohudiri)
Combretum apiculatum
(up to 9 m) (532)
Abundant on rocky, sandy soils; four-
winged seeds are slightly toxic and may
cause hiccupping, but also used
for stomach disorders;
wood is very hard: 1m³
weighs 1 300 kg.

▲ **Large-fruited
Bushwillow**
(Mohudiri)
*Combretum
zeyheri* **(up to 12 m) (546)**
Leaves and seeds rustle in
the winter, hence the
common name in
Afrikaans –
'*raasblaar*'; fibrous
roots are used for basket
weaving; wood is termite and
woodborer-proof, so is used for timber.

Velvet-leaved Bushwillow ▼
(Mohudiri wa lentsure)
Combretum molle **(up to 9 m) (537)**
Pale-yellow, sweetly-scented
flowers occur on spikes;
roots used by local people
for snakebite, stomach
disorders and fever; red dye
is made from leaves.

Narrow-leaved ▼
Turpentine Grass
Cymbopogon plurinodis
(30 cm)

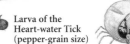

Millipede (Songololo)►
(Sebokolodi)
Doratogonus annulipes
(20 mm)
Scavengers and plant-eaters;
secrete chemicals that give a
distinctive odour to keep
away predators.

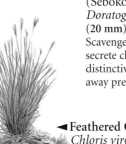

◄**Feathered Chloris**
Chloris virgata **(80 cm)**

◄ **Mountain Aloe** (Mokgopha)
Aloe marlothii **(up to 4 m) (29.5)**
Orange flower-heads produce nectar
popular with sunbirds; leaves used by
local people to make snuff and treat
roundworm and sunburn.

▼ **Khaki Weed**
Tagetes minuta **(up to 2 m)**
Exotic pioneer plant from South
America often found in
disturbed areas; strong-
smelling, black, rice-like seeds
used to make tea; if rubbed on
the skin, the oils are believed to
keep ticks away.

Adults
(F)

Larva of the
Heart-water Tick
(pepper-grain size)

Heart-water Tick (Bont Tick) ▲ ►
Amblyomma hebreaum **(3 - 12 mm)**
Parasitic animals of the Family Ixodidae; similar to insects, but
with eight legs; attach themselves to host, usually a mammal, and
suck blood, becoming grossly bloated before dropping off;
responsible for the transmission of a number of animal diseases.

(M)

GRASSLANDS

In the wet summer months, water runs off surrounding hills and the flatter savannah areas become waterlogged. This ensures enough grass for the large herds of grazers at the end of the season. Grass, like other plants, convert sunlight energy into plant food for a wide variety of grazing animals. Different grass species often grow within an area, and can indicate different soil and drainage patterns. These different grasses in turn support different animal populations that feed on or amongst them.

Fine Thatching Grass►
Hyparrhenia filipendula
(1,5 m)

◄**Sweet-thorn Acacia**
(Mooka)
Acacia karroo
(up to 8 m) (172)
Dark-green, feathery leaves and bright yellow, sweetly-scented pom-pom flowers in midsummer; sickle-shaped pods Apr – Jul; bark exudes an edible gum used in pharmaceutical products; bark also used for tanning leather; flowers produce a great deal of nectar and pollen, attracting many insects; Kori Bustards are attracted by the gum and the insects; leaves and pods are browsed.

◄**Bushveld Shepherds-tree**
(Motlopi) *Boscia foetida*
(up to 5 m) (125)
Inner wood and flowers (Aug – Sept) have rancid smell, hence Afrikaans common name *stinkwitgat*; edible fruit tastes like capers. (See Map, Point 4).

White Buffalo Grass ▲
Panicum coloratum **(1,5 m)**

Orange Tip►
Colotis evenina evenina
(40 - 45 mm)
Stunning orange tips to their wings; favour low-lying, hot areas, but avoid forests and slopes; will fly throughout the year if conditions are right.

 (M)

◄**Leadwood Bushwillow** (Motswere)
Combretum imberbe **(up to 15 m) (539)**
Older trees can be recognised by tall trunk, pale-grey, patterned bark and sparse leaves; small four-winged seeds are pale-green; leaves put on a fire to smoke, will relieve coughs and colds; wood is extremely heavy (1 m³ weighs 1 000 kg); prior to metal, indigenous people used the wood for tools and agricultural implements.

◄ **Looper Moth**
(Serurubele)
Xylopteryx protearia

Gum Grass ▲
Eragrostis gummiflua (**90 cm**)

▼ **Marula** (Morula)
Sclerocarya birrea (**up to 10 m**) (**360**)
In Africa the magic Marula means food, drink, medicine and myth; sweet-smelling fruit, occuring in late summer, is rich in Vitamin C making a refreshing drink, an alchoholic brew, a tasty jelly and jam; elephant do not become intoxicated from eating the fermenting fruit, but baboons, with smaller body weight, may be affected; seeds inside taste like walnuts, and contain oil used in indigenous cosmetics; bark contains anti-hystamine; timber being tough is used for many purposes; roots and leaves are valuable game fodder; Venda people make a bark mixture used to determine the sex of an unborn child. (See Map, Point C7).

◄ **Wool Grass**
Anthephora pubescens (**1,5 m**)

▼ **Umbrella Acacia** (Mosu)
Acacia tortilis (**up to 6 m**) (**188**)
Umbrella shape which usually develops a flat crown as tree gets older; whitish pom-pom flowers appear in midsummer; pods, made up of 20% protein, supply valuable food in winter; bark yields edible gum; pods are used to make necklaces.

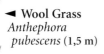

African-wattle (Weeping Wattle) (Mosetlha)►
Peltophorum africanum (**up to 10 m**) (**215**)
Could be mistaken for a thorn tree as it has feathery compound leaves, but no thorns; bears large clusters of bright yellow flowers throughout summer; pods are flat and long, hanging in dense clusters; spittle-bug nymph feeding on sap secretes liquid froth, hence the tree appears to be weeping; rarely browsed as leaves cause the stomach contents to froth; great ecological value as bacteria on roots release nitrogen into soil; said to have magical powers … if your partner dies, and you take a drink made from wattle bark, it will cleanse the blood of your partner.

THICKETS

Many types of trees and shrubs form dense thickets that are important for animals' food and shelter. Taller trees grow in riverine areas, kloofs and gullies where water and soil collect. Tamboti (page 57) thickets are often found on foothills, where soils are more clayey. In eroded streambeds and overgrazed areas Black-thorn Acacia form dense groups. Karree are commonly found growing along water courses.

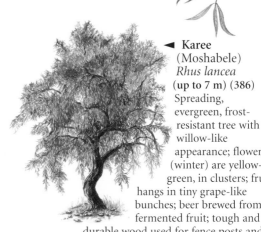

◄ **Karee**
(Moshabele)
Rhus lancea
(**up to 7 m**) (386)
Spreading, evergreen, frost-resistant tree with willow-like appearance; flowers (winter) are yellow-green, in clusters; fruit hangs in tiny grape-like bunches; beer brewed from fermented fruit; tough and durable wood used for fence posts and implement handles.

◄ **Jacket-plum**
(**Indaba Tree**) (Mopepenwe)
Pappea capensis (**up to 10 m**) (433)
Hardy, evergreen tree with rough, leathery leaves; soft, hairy berries which split like a jacket to reveal a soft red seed capsule; fleshy part is browsed; used to make jelly and alcoholic beverage; Cecil John Rhodes and Matabele chief Lobengula, met under one of these trees, hence 'Indaba tree'.

▼ **African Monarch (Milkweed Butterfly)**
Danaus chrysippus aegyptius
(**50 - 70 mm**)
Caterpillars feed on milkweed (Family Asclepiadaceae), which contains a toxic, milky latex; adult butterflies retain this substance; are poisonous to insect-eaters and are thus avoided; occur in most habitats.

(M)

Buffalo-thorn (Mokgalo) ►
Ziziphus mucronata (**up to 9 m**) (447)
Shrub or tree with shiny, fresh-green leaves; paired thorns, one straight, one strongly curved; deciduous, but a few leaves remain in winter; heavily browsed; monkeys, baboons and eland eat the berry-like fruit; local people believe in the magical ability to deflect lightning, and ward off evil spirits; a sacred tree to the Zulus who believe it will wipe out a dead person's spirit, and bury it; has many medicinal uses such as treating infections, dysentery and chest problems.

Black-thorn Acacia (Mongana)
Acacia mellifera (**up to 8 m**) (176)
Tree or shrub forming impenetrable thickets; creamy-white pom-pom flowers in spring; good firewood. (See Map, Point 14).

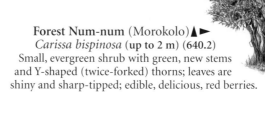

Forest Num-num (Morokolo)▲►
Carissa bispinosa (**up to 2 m**) (640.2)
Small, evergreen shrub with green, new stems and Y-shaped (twice-forked) thorns; leaves are shiny and sharp-tipped; edible, delicious, red berries.

◄**Weeping Faurea**
(**Transvaal Beech**)
(Mofufu/Monyena)
Faurea saligna
(**up to 8 m**) (75)
Also commonly found on hillsides; long, slender leaves on droopy branches, turning red in autumn; white-mauve flowers hang in spikes from Aug – Jan;. (See Map, Point 15).

Kraal Spike-thorn ►
Maytenus polycantha
(**up to 2 m**) (401.2)
Shrub-forming impenetrable thickets used to surround kraals; leaves are small, shiny and grow in clusters; reddish fruit capsules contain yellow seeds.

Finger Grass ►
Digitaria eriantha
(1 m)

▼ **African Olive** (**Wild Olive**) (Motlhare)
Olea europaea/africana (**up to 7 m**) (617)
Common, widespread tree; smooth, shiny dark-green leaves; purple-black, bitter fruits are eaten by animals; wood was used for ornaments; used medicinally to treat colic, and sore eyes and throats.

▼ **Puzzle-bush Stamperwood**
(Morobe)
Ehretia rigida (**up to 4 m**) (657)
Common shrub with tangled appearance; clusters of sweetly-scented, lilac flowers Aug – Feb; branches are used in cattle kraals, as they are believed to subdue bad-tempered oxen; hunters used to believe that pointing these branches at animals will render them weak.

51

ROCKY AREAS

Rocky areas are usually well drained, and rich in nutrients. Water is often available because it collects in the pockets of soil between the rocks. Lavender Croton thrives in this habitat, as does the Large-leaved Rock Fig (page 54), which needs very little soil. Their roots are able to obtain nutrients from the sand in cracks between the rocks.

Some trees have specific nutrient requirements and therefore associate with specific rock types. The Bushveld Red-balloon that is endemic (found nowhere else) to the Pilanesberg area, grows on the red syenite koppies.

▼ **Common Russet Grass**
Loudetia simplex (1,2 m)

▲ **Silky Bushman Grass**
Stipagrostis uniplumis
(75 cm)

Lichens ▼
Can survive extreme conditions very well as are superbly adapted to living on rocks; vulnerable to poisoning by accumulated air pollution; one of oldest plant forms on earth.

◄ **Wild-pear Dombeya
(Common Wild Pear)** (Mokgofa)
Dombeya rotundifolia
(up to 7 m) (471)
Common tree; rough sand-papery leaves; clusters of white or pink flowers appear Jul – Sep; extracts of bark, roots and leaves used for stomach ailments and headaches.

Lavender Croton ►
(Lavender Fever-berry) (Moologa)
Croton gratissimus **(up to 2 m) (328)**
Common tree with elongated leaves, dark-green on top, silver-white dotted with brown underneath; leaves have a lavender fragrance which San women used for perfume.

▼ **Hard Fern**
Pellaea calomelanos
Can survive in exposed, hot, dry places among rocks, by shrivelling up in dry times and rehydrating when it rains; leaves used by local people to soothe nerves and treat colds.

Golden Brown Baboon ►
Spider (Tshere)
Pterinochilus species (60 mm)

▲ **Golden Orb Web Spider**
(Segokgo)
Nephila senegalensis
(25 - 30 mm)

◀ **Wire Grass**
Elionurus muticus (1 m)

▶ Bushveld Red-balloon
Erythrophysa transvaalensis
(**up to 5 m**) (**436.2**)
Quite rare, and can be found on
the red syenite koppies; easiest
to recognise by the balloon-
like, three-angled, fruit
capsules that turn red when
ripe (Oct to Feb); sparsely
branched with a moderate
canopy; once compound leaves have 7 pairs
of leaflets with one at the tip, and a winged
leaf-stalk; unusual and attractive flowers
appear before new leaves in spring. (See
Map, Point 16).

▼ **Yellow Pansy**
Junonia hierta cebrene
(**35 - 40 mm**)
(M)
Visible all year; usually fly close to the
ground, preferring open ground, grassy
spots and gardens; males can be spotted
resting on their territories, usually flat
bare ground, with their wings open.

Highveld Protea (Common Surarbush) ▼
Protea caffra (**2 - 7 m**) (**87**)
Sweet-scented flowers (Nov to Feb) depicted on the
old South African threepenny (ticky) and sixpenny
coins; bark contains tannins; root-bark infusions
used to treat ulcers.

Ants (Ditshoswane) ▼
Family Formicidae
Highly advanced insects; winged male ants die
after mating with queen; workers and soldiers are
sterile; wingless females; often suck aphids for the
sugary sap they secrete, and to protect them from
other insects in return; Matabele Ants can inflict a
painful sting; often seen crossing the road in
columns, returning home after raiding a termite
mound; each ant will carry up to 5 termites; if the
column is disturbed, it emits a high-
pitched buzzing noise.

Bristle-leaved Red Top ▼
Melinis nerviglumis (**1,2 m**)

Snouted Termites (Motlhwa) ▼
Trinervitermes species (**5 - 6 mm**)
Social insects, conspicuous by the large earth mounds
they create above their underground nests; in one
colony there may be millions of inhabitants, all of
whom are the offspring of the single
pair that established it; mounds
vary in size from 35 - 100 cm tall,
and are sealed by a thin shell of
cemented sand.

◀ **Garbage Line Spider**
(Segokgo)
Cyclosa species
(**50 - 150 mm**)

ROCKY AREAS (CONTINUED)

Most of the plants found in Pilanesberg have been utilised by humans over thousands of years. One of the main uses was as natural medicine. Medicinal practises and herbal knowledge has been verbally passed down from generation to generation by traditional healers.

Plants produce different chemicals that allow them to remain healthy and productive. These chemicals, in certain plants, have healing properties that are utilised by healers. Interestingly, the chemical compound in leaves, roots or bark are often quite different – one part may be toxic, while another part completely harmless. The entire plant is very rarely used for medicine.

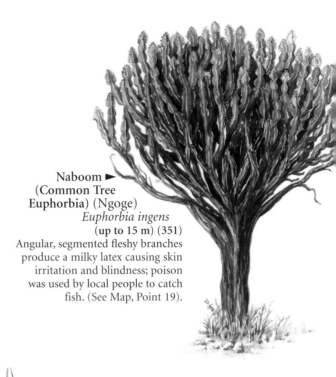

Naboom ▶ (Common Tree Euphorbia) (Ngoge)
Euphorbia ingens
(up to 15 m) (351)
Angular, segmented fleshy branches produce a milky latex causing skin irritation and blindness; poison was used by local people to catch fish. (See Map, Point 19).

Death's Head Hawk ▶ Moth (Serurubele)
Acherontia atropos
(11 cm)

▼ **Mother-in-law's Tongue**
Sansevieria species
Despite its name, is highly prized by man and animal; used in weaving and as a pain-killer, worm remedy and treatment for piles and varicose veins; Black Rhino browse in winter; showy column of flowers; fruits Nov – Feb.

◀**Large-leaved Rock Fig** (Moumo)
Ficus soldanella
(up to 7 m) (63)
The white roots split the rocks open; baboons feed on the fallen figs. (See Map, Point 10).

▼ **Wall Crab Spider (Flattie)** (Segokgo)
Selenops species **(15 - 30 mm)**
Use lightning speed and camouflage to catch food; keep eggs in white disc-shaped web, woven over small depressions in rock face.

Tropical Tent Spider ▶ (Segokgo)
Cyrtophora species
(8 - 20 mm)

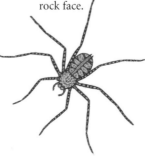

Raisin Bush
Grewia species (**up to 4 m**) (**460, 462**)
Rounded stems; leaves 3 veins from base; yellow flowers produce edible, lobed fruits, reddish when ripe; wood is used for making walking sticks and assegai handles.

Moepel Red-milkwood
Mimusops zeyheri (**3 - 15 m**) (**585**)
Simple glossy, dark lime-green leaves; leaves and orange-yellow fruit enjoyed by elephants, baboons, kudu, duiker and fruit-eating birds; wood used to make farm implements.

Guinea Grass ▶
Panicum maximum
(2,5 m)

◀ Couch Grass
Cynodon dactylon
(45 cm)

Koppie Charaxis ▼
Charaxes jasius saturnus
(75 - 100 mm)
Often seen sucking fluid from elephant dung, or sap of damaged trees; males often visit tops of ridges and koppies at midday; caterpillar's food includes Boer-bean species.

(F)

◀Resurrection Plant (Moswiarula)
Myrothamnus flabellifolius
(20 - 40 cm)
During winter, this green bush seemingly dies, but miraculously springs to life when given water; has many medicinal uses associated with revitalising the body and treating breast diseases; look out for it on the Nkakane Link. (See Map, Point 11).

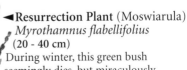

▲ Common Cabbage-tree
Cussonia spicata (**up to 10 m**) (**564**)
Also found on hillslopes; large leaves are dark bluish-green and digitate (hand-like) with deep fissures; bark is cork-like; wood used by Zulu people in treatment of malaria; leaves provide valuable source of fodder.

WATER

Deposits of silt along water courses allow aquatic plants, like reeds, to establish in the water. These plants in turn act as a filter, keeping the water healthy by absorbing excess nutrients and thereby ensuring sufficient oxygen is released in the water. They also provide food and refuge for a variety of animals such as waterbirds, fish and aquatic insects.

Trees that grow along river and drainage lines are evergreen, grow very tall and so are often quite striking. Many of these larger trees have roots securely anchored into the soil in case of flood or heavy river flow. One such tree is the River Bushwillow.

Natal Red Top ▶
Melinis repens (1 m)

◀Blue Buffalo Grass
Cenchrus ciliaris (1 m)

(F)

Brown-veined Migrant ▶
Belenois aurota
(40 - 45 mm)
Visible all year; favour
open country; migrate in
late summer in large numbers
(south-west to north-east).

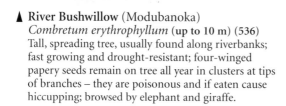

▲ **River Bushwillow** (Modubanoka)
Combretum erythrophyllum (**up to 10 m**) (536)
Tall, spreading tree, usually found along riverbanks;
fast growing and drought-resistant; four-winged
papery seeds remain on tree all year in clusters at tips
of branches – they are poisonous and if eaten cause
hiccupping; browsed by elephant and giraffe.

Hairy Blue Grass ▲
Andropogon chinensis (1,2 m)

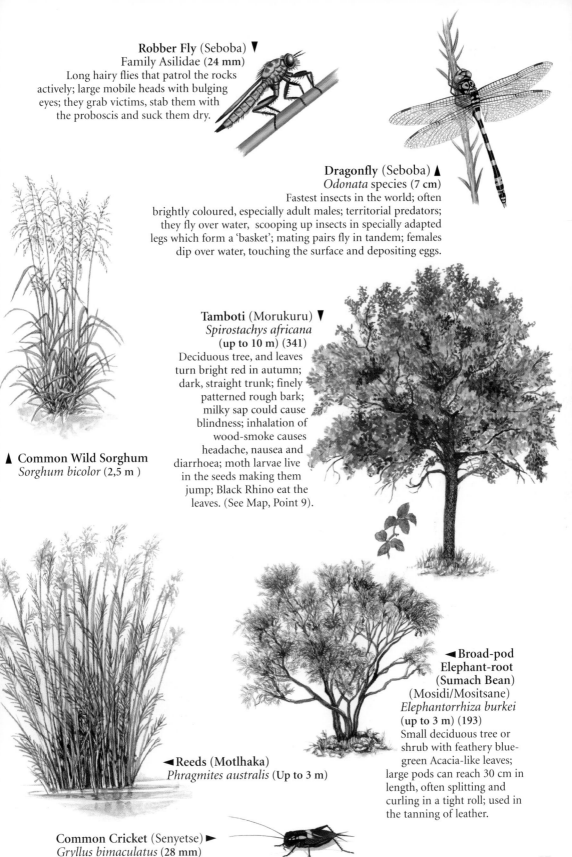

Robber Fly (Seboba) ▼
Family Asilidae (**24 mm**)
Long hairy flies that patrol the rocks
actively; large mobile heads with bulging
eyes; they grab victims, stab them with
the proboscis and suck them dry.

Dragonfly (Seboba) ▲
Odonata species (**7 cm**)
Fastest insects in the world; often
brightly coloured, especially adult males; territorial predators;
they fly over water, scooping up insects in specially adapted
legs which form a 'basket'; mating pairs fly in tandem; females
dip over water, touching the surface and depositing eggs.

Tamboti (Morukuru) ▼
Spirostachys africana
(**up to 10 m**) (**341**)
Deciduous tree, and leaves
turn bright red in autumn;
dark, straight trunk; finely
patterned rough bark;
milky sap could cause
blindness; inhalation of
wood-smoke causes
headache, nausea and
diarrhoea; moth larvae live
in the seeds making them
jump; Black Rhino eat the
leaves. (See Map, Point 9).

▲ **Common Wild Sorghum**
Sorghum bicolor (**2,5 m**)

◄**Broad-pod
Elephant-root
(Sumach Bean)**
(Mosidi/Mositsane)
Elephantorrhiza burkei
(**up to 3 m**) (**193**)
Small deciduous tree or
shrub with feathery blue-
green Acacia-like leaves;
large pods can reach 30 cm in
length, often splitting and
curling in a tight roll; used in
the tanning of leather.

◄**Reeds** (Motlhaka)
Phragmites australis (**Up to 3 m**)

Common Cricket (Senyetse) ►
Gryllus bimaculatus (**28 mm**)

57

HISTORY

HUMANS AND NATURE

Many people say that the Garden of Eden lay in Africa, a natural paradise where people and animals lived side by side. History was born here, and for millions and millions of years, humans and animals co-existed, changing and surviving within the protection of the ancient volcano. Today, this is still so, and the story continues to unfold.

Middle Stone Age

Between 20 0000 and 40 000 years ago, a new age began – the spine of prehistoric man had straightened. We call these people *Homo sapiens*. They had developed more advanced tools, like sharp stone points and flake blades. To increase their safety and comfort, they took shelter in caves, and lit fires against the freezing cold. This period saw the last Ice Age cover the Earth in frozen snows and glaciers.

By then, *Homo sapiens* had become skilled hunters. The common hunting technique was to drive game into pit traps. There is evidence that by the end of this period, a number of animal species had already been hunted into extinction by humans.

Skull showing
Sabre-toothed Tiger
tooth marks

Early Stone Age

2,5 million years ago, our early ancestors invented the first tools – crude hand axes, choppers, irregular cutting flakes, and later, multi-purpose axes and cleavers. This development was as important then, as landing on the moon is to us now.

This period lasted for 2 million years. Early people depended solely on their environment and on their own growing intelligence. They gathered food or scavenged for it, but had not yet learned to hunt large game. Like many of the animals, they were the prey of predators like the Sabre-toothed Tiger. But unlike other mammals, stone age people ran on two legs and had the use of their hands.

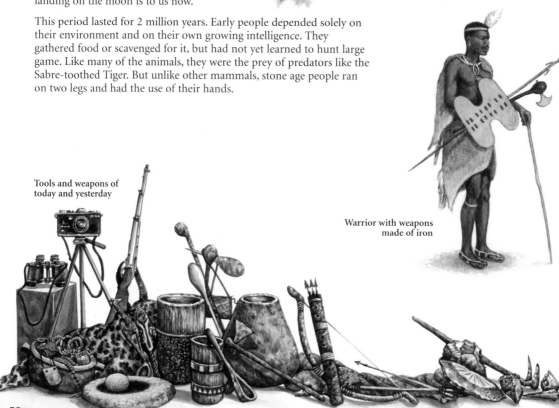

Tools and weapons of
today and yesterday

Warrior with weapons
made of iron

Late Stone Age

This period occurred between 40 000 BC and 300 AD. It is associated with the Bushman (San) who were hunter-gatherers, and the Khoikhoi (Hottentot) who were stock herders of cattle and goats. About 6 000 years ago, the climate became much warmer, making survival easier. This was assisted by the development of new tools, like the scraper, and of course the bow and arrow. The San were very skilled hunters. With this new technology, they had time for leisure and time to think. They painted on rocks and made engravings, telling the stories of their lives and their religious beliefs. There are some fine examples of rock art in the Park, but they are well off the beaten track.

San hunters with bows and arrows

Remains of skeletons and graves in the area show that ochre, symbolic of blood, was used for burials. This ritual was possibly one of the first religious sparks in human history.

The San lived a nomadic existence, following game and rainfall across the vast African plains. Rain meant life. Drought often meant death. Rain gods were invoked through trance dances. Similar rituals were later practiced by Ba-Tswana people who built shrines to the rain god. Such shrines have been found in Pilanesberg.

Early Iron Age

In about 300 AD, huge changes swept the sub-continent. Bantu-speaking people arrived from the north with new ways and a new technology. This transformed the area forever. They brought crops and the knowledge of iron. They also smelted copper and gold, made pottery and kept domestic stock. A new concept was born – the acquisition of wealth.

Village with animal kraal

For the first time, humans took more than just their basic needs from nature, and this placed significant stress on the environment. Iron smelting needed charcoal, and there was plenty of this to be found in the dense woodlands and forests. In addition, bush had to be cleared to make way for crops like cow-peas, sorghum, millet and ground beans. Society revolved around keeping goats and cattle, and villages were built around the animal kraals. To enter the village, visitors would first walk through the kraal to see the wealth and strength of the chief and his people. Basic survival was now softened by the security of wealth.

Climatically, this period was one of see-sawing change. From 100 - 200 AD it was colder than it is today, but it warmed up again between 200 - 600 AD. Then again, a much colder period took over between 600 - 900 AD. These changes affected the movement of people. They settled when conditions were good, and moved away when it was too dry or too cold.

Despite their greater security, people were still dependent on nature. They moved with the changes of climate and season, and with the movement of game. They still obeyed nature's laws, but they had learned to use it to their advantage.

HISTORY

HUMANS AND NATURE
(CONTINUED)

Late Iron Age

Between 1 000 AD and the 1830s, the population in the
western Transvaal area increased significantly. Inevitable
conflict lay ahead. The first half of this millennium was
characterised by settlements on foothills of mountains.
From about 1 600 AD, large stone structures were built on
the tops of hills, from where enemies could be seen
easily, and the village better defended. Huge 'mega-sites'
(1 - 3 kilometres across), housing up to 20 000 people, sprung up on large, open
areas in the western Transvaal. Such a site can be seen at Malokwane, south-west of the
Pilanesberg. Within Pilanesberg however, smaller sites were built on foothills. From here
a village had good views, but at the same time, was well hidden from enemies. There
were no 'mega-sites' in Pilanesberg. This meant less stress on the environment.

Pilanesberg has seen times of violence and great turbulence

Between 1400 and 1850, climatic changes occurred once again – a cold, dry period (the
Little Ice Age) was followed by warmer, wetter conditions. Around 1800, flooding rains and much
higher temperatures brought prosperity to the land and people.

With more and more people entering the western Transvaal, it was not long before competition for
resources shattered the peace. The late 18th and early 19th Century was a time of great turbulence
and violence. Sometimes known as the Mfecane, or the 'scattering', this time saw many chiefdoms and
people move around within South Africa. New chiefdoms moved into the western Transvaal area.

The Bakgatla

Between 1700 and 1750, the Bakgatla people established themselves near present-day Saulspoort (at the
northern tip of the Park). They belonged to the Setswana linguistic group. Under the leadership of chief
Masselane, they trekked from Hammanskraal, near present day Pretoria. But the new pastures were ruled by
the Batlhako tribe, and for a while the Bakgatla had to pay tribute to
live there. When they refused to continue payment, war broke
out. The Bakgatla won and enjoyed some years of
dominance in the area.

Pilanesberg is named after the Bakgatla chief,
Pilane, who ruled between 1825 and 1850.
No one could have risen to power at a
more difficult time, because in 1825,
the Ndebele warlord, Mzilikaze, swept
into the region. He brought
turbulence and terror, subduing
Pilane's people, imposing taxes and
forcing them to look after his cattle.
Mzilikaze's war parties caused havoc
throughout the western Transvaal.
With so many corpses littering the
bushveld, lions developed a taste for
human flesh.

Huts were built on platforms or in
trees to be safe from marauding lions.

Early Stone Age 2 500 000 - 200 000 BC

Pilanesberg's
Historical
Time-line
1 mm = 2 000 years

60

Arrival of Settlers from Europe

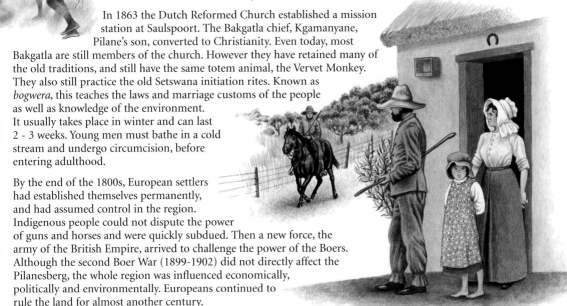

Around this time missionaries and European settlers began to move into the area. Mzilikaze did not tolerate their presence, except for one extraordinary case. To this day, it remains a fascinating story – the missionary, Robert Moffat entered the region in 1829. He and the Ndebele warlord struck up an instant friendship. Other trespassers were violently chased out but Mzilikaze regarded Moffat as a friend, and even a brother.

Mzilikaze's reign of terror lasted until a combined force of Ba-Tswana, Griqua and European settlers drove him out. This was not the first, or last time, that black and white settlers joined to oust a common enemy. The Ndebele fled to southern Zimbabwe and established themselves in Bulawayo.

In 1863 the Dutch Reformed Church established a mission station at Saulspoort. The Bakgatla chief, Kgamanyane, Pilane's son, converted to Christianity. Even today, most Bakgatla are still members of the church. However they have retained many of the old traditions, and still have the same totem animal, the Vervet Monkey. They also still practice the old Setswana initiation rites. Known as *bogwera*, this teaches the laws and marriage customs of the people as well as knowledge of the environment. It usually takes place in winter and can last 2 - 3 weeks. Young men must bathe in a cold stream and undergo circumcision, before entering adulthood.

By the end of the 1800s, European settlers had established themselves permanently, and had assumed control in the region. Indigenous people could not dispute the power of guns and horses and were quickly subdued. Then a new force, the army of the British Empire, arrived to challenge the power of the Boers. Although the second Boer War (1899-1902) did not directly affect the Pilanesberg, the whole region was influenced economically, politically and environmentally. Europeans continued to rule the land for almost another century.

By the end of the 1800s, European settlers had established themselves.

Further Influences

Over this last century, cycles of conflict and resolution, and the rapid advance in technology, have left their mark on the Pilanesberg. The most dramatic effect on the environment came from mechanised agriculture, large herds of domestic stock, and huge hunting expeditions. This saw the gradual disappearance of wild animals, and the temporary destruction of natural habitats.

Smaller influences on the environment had always occurred. For instance Iron Age communities planted Euphorbia trees around their homes. These were regarded as magical and medicinal trees, and can still be seen at old village sites in the Park.

A direct influence of nature on humans came from the surface water in Pilanesberg. Volcanic rock formations here contain large amounts of fluoride. This is taken up in the water and causes the teeth of long-term inhabitants in the area to go brown (dental fluorosis). At one time, it was said that they could not believe the pure white teeth of newcomers to the area. Today water is piped in from other sources.

The most dramatic influence that humans and nature have had on each other in the Pilanesberg, happened very recently. For the first time in the area, people came to assist nature, and not only use it for their own benefit.

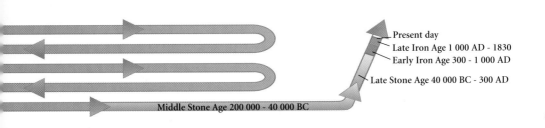

Present day
Late Iron Age 1 000 AD - 1830
Early Iron Age 300 - 1 000 AD

Late Stone Age 40 000 BC - 300 AD

Middle Stone Age 200 000 - 40 000 BC

61

HISTORY

CREATION AND CONSERVATION

Creating the Pilanesberg Park has been a long and complicated process. Since its birth in 1979, dedicated people have nurtured and nourished it. Today it still requires huge effort, careful planning and a vision of the future.

By the year 2 000 AD, some 80 million eco-tourists, worldwide, will visit places like Pilanesberg every year. As more and more of us enjoy the outdoors, we have to ask– can nature sustain itself, as well as us? And how can we give it a helping hand?

These pages show that Pilanesberg is a managed system, involving veld, animal and people management. This is the way to ensure future generations will also benefit from our natural heritage.

Park History

Pilanesberg Park was first conceived in 1969. It took ten years of research and legislation before it finally opened on 8 December 1979. But before it could be stocked with game, the 55 000 hectare area had to be prepared.

The first step was to remove all evidence of mechanised farming and mining. Houses, fences, windmills, pumps and mining equipment were dismantled and trucked away. Tons of alien vegetation were removed, and indigenous vegetation was seeded in its place. The battle to reclaim eroded land began. Eventually, the area was fenced and Operation Genesis began.

Generously funded by the South African Nature Foundation, and many other organisations, this operation remains the largest game translocation in the world. 5 957 animals of 19 different species were initially moved in from parks across southern Africa. Even the fabled Noah did not have to contend with 50 elephants, 1 937 impala, or 19 critically endangered Black Rhino, to mention a few. Due to veterinary restrictions, most animals were quarantined in a 1 200 hectare boma, before final release.

Translocating animals to and from Pilanesberg continues. So does the management of these animals and the habitats in which they live. In addition, management must take care of approximately 120 000 visitors a year.

Constant research and monitoring of animals helps keep a sustainable natural balance in the Park.

Veterinary control prevents disease.

People Management

Large numbers of visitors could have a negative impact on the Park. But revenue from tourism also keeps the Park alive. A delicate balance is therefore needed between people and the Pilanesberg. Looking after visitors includes the building and maintainance of roads, hides, picnic and view sites. This is an ongoing task aimed at making your visit more enjoyable.

Law enforcement is very important. Respecting the Park's laws allows management to get on with looking after the animals and their habitats.

Veld Management

Conserving habitat is of vital importance. Without their habitats, no animals would survive. A few aspects of veld management are outlined here.

- Erosion is controlled by building rock packs, gabions, contour drains, dams and weirs. This prevents valuable soil being washed away.
- Most of Pilanesberg is covered in unpalatable sourveld. Veld burning is necessary as it encourages palatable grass to grow.
- Alien plants which are poisonous to game and destructive to natural habitats, are always being removed.
- Good veld management is the basis of good animal management.

Springbok grazing new grass. (see page 17)

Translocation of animals to and from Pilanesberg is an ongoing process.

Animal Management

Today it is said that animals must 'pay their way' if they are to survive in such a full and competitive world. Wildlife must benefit people, and people must benefit wildlife. Here are a few points that help to ensure this:

- Excess game is translocated to other parks. In 1994, Pilanesberg sold 19 White Rhino for R361 000. This money benefits the Park and the people living around it.
- A game census is conducted every year. If there are too many animals, some must be culled. This prevents the destruction of habitats.
- Veterinary control prevents disease.
- Scout patrols guard against poachers and check that fences are intact.

Looking after our natural heritage is a 24-hour-a-day job for the Park's management team. But it is important to realise that by being here, and obeying the laws, you too are making a positive difference. Thank you for keeping Pilanesberg beautiful.

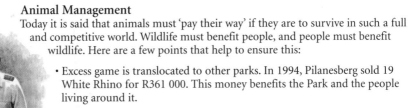

PILANESBERG MAP

The road network through the Park affords access to a wide variety of habitats. This improves the chances of seeing the broad spectrum of fauna and flora that this diverse region offers.

All Hides and Picnic Spots are equipped with toilets and are safely fenced. Picnic Spots also offer braai facilities, water and shade. Most Points of Discovery and Viewsites do not have facilities and are not fenced. Please do not get out unless the area is fenced and it is safe to do so.

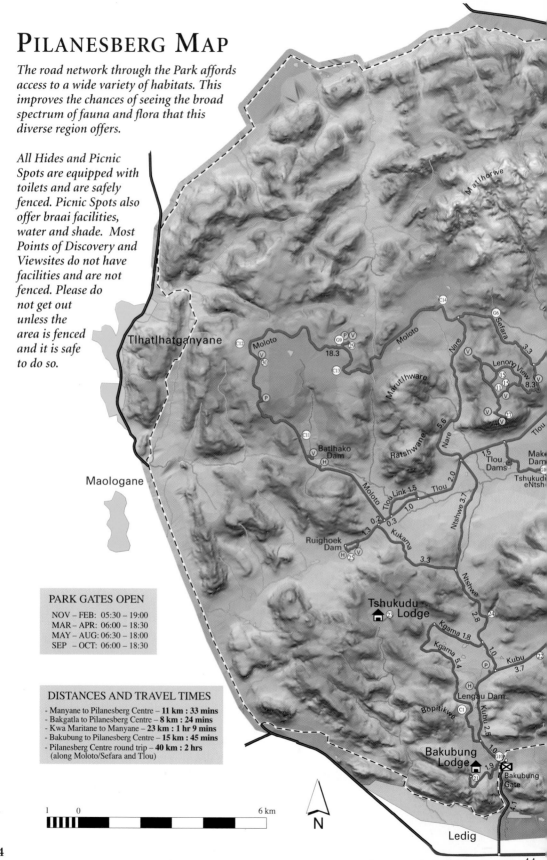

PARK GATES OPEN

NOV – FEB: 05:30 – 19:00
MAR – APR: 06:00 – 18:30
MAY – AUG: 06:30 – 18:00
SEP – OCT: 06:00 – 18:30

DISTANCES AND TRAVEL TIMES

- Manyane to Pilanesberg Centre – **11 km : 33 mins**
- Bakgatla to Pilanesberg Centre – **8 km : 24 mins**
- Kwa Maritane to Manyane – **23 km : 1 hr 9 mins**
- Bakubung to Pilanesberg Centre – **15 km : 45 mins**
- Pilanesberg Centre round trip – **40 km : 2 hrs**
  (along Moloto/Sefara and Tlou)

Tlhatlhatganyane

Maologane

Matlhorwe

Moloto

Sefara 3.3

Lenong View 8.3

Moloto 18.3

Marutlhware

Nare

Nare 5.6

Tlou

Ratshwane

1.5 Tlou Dams

Make Dam

Tshukudi eNtsh

Batlhako Dam

Moloto

Tlou Link 1.5

Tlou 1.5

Tlou 1.0

Ntshwe 3.7

Ntshwe 2.0

0.2

0.3

1.3

Kukama

Ruighoek Dam

3.3

Ntshwe 2.8

24

Tshukudu Lodge

Kgama 1.8

Kgama 5.4

1.0

Kubu 3.7

Lengau Dam

Bopitikwe

Kubu 2.5

1.0

Bakubung Lodge

1.9

Bakubung Gate

4.1

Ledig

N

1   0   6 km

4.4

POINTS OF DISCOVERY

Discovering Pilanesberg can be more than just a glimpse of one, two, or (if you are lucky) three of the Big Five. The Map will help you find unusual and interesting features. From the fascinating world of insects, to magical and medicinal trees, these Discovery Points provide the clues as to where and why and how it all happens in Pilanesberg.

PLEASE NOTE AS YOU DRIVE ALONG:

- The Discovery Points are divided into:
  - General (points 1 - 33)
  - Cultural/Historical (points C1 - C20)
  - Geological (points G1 - G15) (see pages 4/5)
- The points are not necessarily in numerical order; some numbers are repeated at more than one place.
- Look around carefully as not all points are right next to the road.

GENERAL POINTS OF DISCOVERY

1   Manyane Complex

- **North West Parks & Tourism Board Headquarters**
  Tel: (014) 555-5351/2/3/4 Fax: (014) 555-5525
  E-mail: nwptb@iafrica.com
  Web: www.tourismnorthwest.co.za

- **Manyane**
  - Self-catering and time share chalets
  - Caravan park with 100 fully-electrified caravan stands, 60 camping sites, ablution & laundry facilities
  - A lá carte restaurant, shop & bar
  - Swimming pool, jungle gym, mini-golf and walk-in aviary (over 80 species of indigenous birds)
  - Bosele Camp with dormitories; fully catered (for school groups of up to 204 children)
    Tel: (014) 555-6135/9 Fax: (014) 555-6122

2   Walking Area (Self-guided Trails)

Stretch your legs and enjoy nature at close range, by experiencing the Walking Area at Manyane. This area is fenced and has no large, dangerous animals. A route map and guide to interesting features is available. This offers environmental education while enjoying game viewing or bird watching on foot.

3   Salty Spring

A mineral hotspot, known as Letswaana, that provides animals with vital nutrients all year long. It was also a cattle outpost linked to Lerome village.

4   Bushveld Shepherds-tree Area

The unusual *Boscia foetida* or 'Stinkwitgat' is drought resistant. It gets its name from the pungent smell of the flowers and inner wood. The edible fruit tastes like capers.

5   Malatse Hide – Fenced

A site showing management's efforts to restore nature and to provide visitors with rewarding viewing. The weir and man-made dam prevent erosion and have encouraged wildlife back to this dry part of the Park. Sable, eland and rhino may be among the rewards for patient viewers.

6 Gully Thickets

Remnants of ancient forests survive where two hillsides meet. These gullies collect water and soil, and the denser vegetation provides good habitat for leopard, bushbuck, kudu and a wealth of forest birds.

7 Bakgatla

- Manyane style brick chalets set in attractive mountains
- Full facilities & swimming pool
- Braai & picnic sites with kiosk, ablutions & children's playground
- Camping

Tel: (014) 555-6135/9
Fax: (014) 555-6122

8 Ratlhogo Hide – Fenced

An excellent hide to watch game coming down to drink, mud-rollers enjoying a wallow, terrapin and birds. The karree trees are indicative of wet areas. Thick bush provides good cover for kudu, bushbuck, waterbuck and other woodland species.

9 Tamboti Circle

Black Rhino and porcupine enjoy these highly poisonous trees, but smoke of burning wood causes nausea and headaches in humans. In Nov-Jan look out for Tamboti 'jumping beans' – the larvae of a small grey moth spasmodically stretching inside the Tamboti seeds.

10 Large-leaved Rock Figs

Look high on the cliffside to see the rock fig taking root in rocks, splitting them with their geotropic (earth-seeking) force. Their white roots are distinctive on many rocky areas throughout the Park.

11 Resurrection Plant

A hardy plant that appears dead in dry times, but a little water brings it to miraculous life. It is a good-luck plant, and is also used to cleanse the blood of a very sick person.

General Points of Discovery (continued)

12 Flat Rock and Natural Seep

A natural seep causes permanent water to collect and attracts game to this area.

13 Termite Mounds

These small, rounded mounds have been created by the genus Hodotermes. This is the first step to rehabilitation, as termites eat the dead wood from felled trees, and soon birds and game return to lengthen the food chain.

14 Black-thorn Acacia Area

Indicative of nutritious Sweetveld, these *Acacia mellifera* trees are excellent fodder for browsers. Grass is sometimes lacking in Sweetveld as it is well utilised by grazers. In old times, these trees were used to form kraals or to snare fish driven down a narrow stream.

15 Weeping Faurea (Transvaal Beech)

These fire-resistant trees are indicative of Sourveld which does not provide much nutrition in winter. Due to the accumulation of dry, unpalatable grasses, Sourveld burns very easily. A red dye is made from these *Faurea saligna* trees.

16 Bushveld Red-balloon

This extremely rare plant, *Erythrophysa transvaalensis*, occurs only in syenite koppies. It can be seen above the drilled rocks at G7, growing almost out of the rock. This tree is protected in South Africa.

17 Mankwe Lake View Platform – Fenced

Situated in the centre of Pilanesberg, this spot offers excellent viewing, especially of waterbirds. The domed hills bear testament to volcanic activity, pushed out through plugs in the earth's crust. Crocodile and hippo rule the water and birds come to breed and feed nearby.

18 Animal Off-loading Ramp

In 1979 this ramp was used extensively in "Operation Genesis", the largest translocation of game to date. The many species of game introduced into the park have flourished over the past 22 years.

19 Naboom (Euphorbia)

A cactus-like plant, the *Euphorbia ingens*, is enjoyed by Black Rhino. The San used it to make poison arrows and its milky latex can blind people. Some say the tree is a protection against lightning. They are often home to genets and bushbabies.

20 Fish Eagle Picnic Site – Fenced

The superb view, variety of trees, distinctive rocks and the interface of 3 habitats (rocky outcrop, hillside and water) make this attractive area a haven for wildlife. It was once an Iron Age kraal site, being easily defendable and close to water. Trees include Acacias, Bushwillows, Tamboti and Marula.

21 *Bakubung*

LEGACY
HOTELS & RESORTS

- Superb hotel accommodation overlooking private dam with resident hippos
- Bar area, restaurant, curio shop, conference centre & sporting facilities
- Afternoon, sunrise & sundowner game drives & bush braais
- Guided bush trails

Tel: (014) 552-6000
Fax: (014) 552-6161

22 Wagon Tracks

From a century ago these tracks have left their mark in the ouklip rock. Ouklip is formed when water evaporates leaving minerals behind. On the other side of the road on the far slope, are lines of trees – evidence of an old orchard. Indigenous trees have taken advantage of the old orchard holes.

24 Brown Hyaena Area

These shy, nocturnal animals are seldom seen, but keep a sharp lookout, especially on a night drive, because their lair is hidden nearby in the safety of the rocky hillsides. White middens (heaps of dung used as territorial markers) may often be seen next to the road.

LEGACY
HOTELS & RESORTS

23 TSHUKUDU

- 6 luxury thatched chalets, nestled against an isolated koppie and overlooking its own waterhole with superb game viewing
- Five star standards
- Game drives and walks accompanied by a ranger

Tel: (014) 552-6255
Fax: (014) 552-6266

25 Ruighoek Dam

A natural catchment area, surrounded by 4 prominent habitats – water, hillside, grassland and woodland. As a result many species occur, especially those dependent on water. A wide variety of trees including Karee, African Olive, Shepherds-tree and Buffalo-thorn Jubube make this an excellent area for birds and game.

26 Makorwane Dam – Hide

Another diversity of habitat with grassland, hills, rocky outcrops and water. Primary grassland and sweet thorn trees are the first stage of indigenous vegetation re-establishing on old farmlands. Note aloes on the hill and flooded trees which are good nesting sites. Dams help to recreate well-balanced water habitats.

27 Lenong View

Named after the vulture, this panoramic view sheds light on the Pilanesberg volcano. The mountains were once boiling magma, pushed up through concentric cracks in the earth's crust. These are called ring dykes, exposed to us through weathering. Scars of old farmland are evident in erosion and open, recovering grassland. Natural processes assisted by management rehabilitate the area. The mountain top is Sourveld where Weeping Faurea, Resurrection Plant, Highveld Protea and Rock Figs grow. Mountain Reedbuck, eland and gemsbok can be found here.

28 Macrotermes Termite Mound

This mound has been created by the genus *Macrotermes*. This termite is renowned for building extremely large mounds, some of which are taller than 1,8 m. These termites contribute to the ecosystem by advancing the decomposition process of dead wood.

29 Moloto Picnic – Fenced

Mountains and rocky outcrops are home to baboon, klipspringer, leopard and large raptors. Good grassland nearby is where buffalo, reedbuck, giraffe and lion can be seen. This interface of 2 habitats draws a wide variety of species, especially birds.

30 Moloto Plain

A spectacular view of grasslands, rocky outcrops, hillsides, water and woodlands. Animals like White Rhino, wildebeest, springbok, zebra and cheetah can be seen on the plain. A wide variety of trees germinate and seed easily in rocky areas where water and soil collect.

31 Rhino Rubbing Post

Some posts in the Park are smooth from years of White Rhino enjoying a good rub to remove parasites from their skin.

33 Iron Age Walling

Walls can be seen throughout Pilanesberg. They date back to the 17th Century when Batswana settlements sprung up throughout the Western Transvaal. Small villages were built at the base of hills so that look-outs could be easily posted without enemies detecting the village. Some may even have belonged to the infamous Matabele chief, Mzilikaze.

32 *Kwa Maritane* Place of the Rock

LEGACY
HOTELS & RESORTS

- Luxurious hotel & timeshare game lodge, 5 bed luxury duplex cabanas or 8-bed chalets with private patios
- Conference centre, bar & restaurant overlooking illuminated waterhole
- Underground viewing hide
- Two swimming pools; tennis and volleyball courts
- Day and night game drives; bush braais

Tel: (014) 552-5100
Fax: (014) 552-5333

CULTURAL/HISTORICAL POINTS OF DISCOVERY

C1 Totem Animals

Totemism has long been a feature of the Tswana culture and refers to the veneration of an animal, plant or object. Each Tswana clan associated themselves with a specific totem animal, e.g. Bakubung tribe: hippo; Bakgatla tribe: monkey. Many existing myths and legends explain why certain totems were adopted. Association with a particular totem carried with it certain responsibilities and traditions. Should a member not act according to the rules, that person would have to undergo a purification ceremony to prevent misfortune.

C2 Borite Hill

View of Borite Hill, a large flat rock, known as Letlapa la Kgamanyane. The hillside to the east was the location of the original Mabele-a-Podi village of kgosi Pilane who oversaw the reunification of the Bakgatla after the disruptions caused by the *difiqane*.

C3 Kgotla

The *Kgotla* or meeting place of kgosi Pilane was situated below Borite Hill. It was close to a well used by the Bakgatla Royal family. From this imposing rock kgosi Pilane addressed his army prior to embarking in war.

C4 Initiation cleansing site

Despite efforts by Christian missionaries, rituals and ceremonies such as *bogwera* (circumcision for boys) and *bojale* (for girls) still formed an important part of Bakgatla culture. This rocky outcrop, with several overhanging rocks and a hidden fountain, provided shelter for a ritual cleansing for initiates returning from initiation school prior to going back to the village.

C5 Initiation school

Located in this valley, secluded from the village, the initiation schools were held, both for boys (left) and girls (right).

C6 Execution Koppie

The steep rock, locally known as Slagterskop, was used for executions by throwing a person off the rock, after a Lekgotla held at kgosi Pilane's kraal had found them guilty. Beehives are found in caves on this hill, yet the honey was never harvested or used.

C7 Marula trees

The Marula trees in this area were used as location for general tribal meetings – Lekgotla – giving the area its name of Marula wa Phala. The magic Marula means food, drink, medicine and myth in Africa.

C8 Sacred hill

The hill to the south-west of the road, known as Thaba ya Ditshwene, is sacred to the Bakgatla. It is rumoured that in the early evenings there were sounds of voices, cattle lowing and smoke rising from this hill despite no people residing at or visiting the hill. A ceremony was held by elders in 1979, during which the ancestral spirits were moved, resulting in the hill falling strangely silent.

C9 Sacred hill

Located close to the first settlement of the Bakgatla in the Pilanesberg, this hill was used for sacred rituals such as rain-making.

C10 Plains

Old women, unable to work in the fields, often visited this area to collect grasses favoured for weaving, e.g. Love Grass (*Eragrostis curvula*) and Gum Grass (*Eragrostis gummiflua*). The shape of women harvesting the grass from these plains possibly gave the place its name of Mampye – place of the ostrich.

C11 Dutch Reformed Church Site

Boer expropriation of Bakgatla land during the 1830s to 1840s, left the tribe generally landless. The inability to buy land in their own name, resulted in the formation of strategic alliances between the Bakgatla and missionaries such as HL Gonin, of the Dutch Reformed Church. During the 1860s kgosi Kgamanyane invited Gonin to work among the Bakgatla, possibly for political, economic and security purposes due to the problems they faced from the local Boers. The Bakgatla's first farms were bought with Gonin's assistance – Saulspoort was the largest.

C12 Securing tenure

Besides the farm Saulspoort, the Reverend Gonin purchased Welgeval (1864), Skaapkraal (1867) and half of Koedoesfontein in 1891. In 1898 Saulspoort was sold to the Bakgatla. In 1912, Welgeval farm was sold by to group of 9 individuals, including kgosi Ramono, and a relatively wealthy farmer, C Sefara. This provided security of tenure to the group of buyers, most of whom had been living on this farm since the 1880s.

Skaapkraal was held in trust for the Bakgatla under Tidimane Ramono Pilane through a sale from CBS Harmse to the Minister of Native Affairs in 1950.

C13 Welgeval/Skaapkraal border

Farm boundaries were marked with stone cairns, some of which are still visible, and known by elders of the Bakgatla clan. Foundations and ruins of early villages are also visible.

C14 Driefontein Farm

A large degree of close socio-economic co-operation and interdependence existed between the Bakgatla and white farmers in the Pilanesberg. Elders from the Bakgatla remember working on the farms in the 1930s, assisting in harvesting, and being paid one bag of oranges for a Saturday's work, at the Driefontein Farm.

C15 Sephikile village

Situated on the farm Spitskop, this was home to the teacher-evangelist K Makgale for some 65 years, starting in 1897. A quartz mine for glass manufacturing was established on the hill behind the village site. Following the South African War, the Bakgatla had a lot of cattle, enabling them to purchase the farm Spitzkop 298 from the Cyferbult Trading Company for £400. Ironically most of the cattle were looted from the Boers who had dispossessed the Bakgatla of lands in the 1840s.

C16 European Farm school

Despite numerous schools being established in Pilanesberg – all by mission societies with emphasis on Bible teaching – the Bakgatla were becoming increasingly dissatisfied with the curriculum, resulting in the establishment of the successful Ramalope School in Saulspoort. Unlike the European school that was established here, Government only supported education in the region toward the end of the 1930s when it took over Ramalope School and renamed it Ofentse School (currently a cultural heritage museum).

C17 Boer settlement

After the arrival of Boer settlers in the Pilanesberg in 1837, relations between the Bakgatla and Boers deteriorated from being mutually co-operative to outright hostile. This happened after Commandant Paul Kruger flogged kgosi Kgamanyane at Saulspoort for refusing to provide labour for an irrigation project.

During the South African War, the Bakgatla backed the British, and embarked on their own Bakgatla-Boer war. Initially a few Boer farmers returned to Pilanesberg, under protection of local South African Constabulary units. Bakgatla terror kept most Boer farms unoccupied until after World War 1. Boer settler farmstead ruins are visible, as are signs of terracing, roads, woodlots and graves.

C18 Bakhari shop

For a long time this was the only shop in the area. As a general dealer, it was the attraction for all and sundry.

C19 Pilanesberg Centre

Originally built as a magistrates court in 1936, it was frequented by the Bakgatla to obtain passes and identity documents, as well as register marriages, births and deaths. It has been converted into a restaurant and curio shop. Enjoy breakfast, lunch and tea from the terrace of this finely preserved building.

C20 Houwater

Originally known as Houwater, the area around the dam was extensively utilised for agriculture. The deep soils and proximity of water allowed for ploughing and extensive agricultural development. In 1963 the transfer of the farm to the South African Bantu Development Trust took place.

GLOSSARY

aphid – a tiny insect (bug) that lives on plants, causing them harm

aphrodisiac – a substance that arouses sexual desire

aquatic – an animal or plant that lives in water

arid – an area of insufficient water to support lush vegetation

bachelor herd – a herd of male antelope that do not hold a breeding herd territory of their own

barometer – an instrument that measures atmospheric pressure

bosses – the hard projection on the front of the head or horns of some animals

breeding herd – a herd of female antelope in season, kept together by a dominant male that mates with each female

browser – an animal that mainly eats leaves

camouflage – a method of disguising or concealing animals by their colouring

carcass – the dead body of an animal

carnivorous/carnivore – an animal that eats meat

carrion – the meat of a dead animal (sometimes rotten)

carrying capacity – the maximum number of animals an area can hold without causing damage to that area

catchment area – an area from which rain drains into a river or dam

census – an official count of the animal population

cere – the bare coloured skin at the base of bill of a bird of prey

chiefdoms – an area controlled by one chief

colony – birds that breed together in large groups

conserving – keeping from harm or loss, for future use

contour drain – a man-made furrow which channels water & helps prevent soil wash away

courtship display – the behaviour shown by animals while trying to attract their sexual partners

crust – the rocky outer layer of the earth's surface

crustacean – an animal that has a hard shell

cytotoxin – a poison that destroys the body's tissue

deciduous – a plant that loses its leaves during winter

dewlap – a fold of skin that hangs from the throat of some animals e.g. eland

diurnal – an animal that is active during the day

eco-tourist – someone who travels to wildlife destinations on holiday

endangered – species that are in danger of becoming extinct, & usually protected by law

engravings – art that is cut or carved into a hard surface like stone

excrement – the waste matter discharged from the bowels

exoskeleton – the external bony or leathery covering of an animal

extinction – the final loss of an entire species that will never exist in living form again

fault – a break in the earth's layers of rock caused by movement of the earth's crust

forage – to search for food

gabions – rocks that are packed together in wire mesh, in order to prevent soil being washed away

gape – the angle at base of bill where upper & lower parts of the mouth meet

glaciers – a river of ice that moves very slowly

gradient – the steepness of a hill or mountain

grazers – animals that mainly eat grass & roots

gregarious – living in social groups

habitat – the natural environment of an animal or plant

hierarchy – a system that ranks one animal above another

indigenous – plants that are native to an area ie. were not brought in from another area

initiation – a special ceremony that admits a person into the society as an adult

insectivorous/insectivore – an animal that eats insects

invasive – plants that spread easily into an area where they are not wanted

kraal – an enclosure for goats, sheep and cattle

larva – an insect, from time of leaving egg, until changing into pupa

latex – the milky liquid in the stems & leaves of certain plants

linguistic group – a group of people who speak the same language

matriarch – a female that is the leader of her herd, pride or flock

migrant – a bird that moves to warmer areas when it gets cold & food is scarce

millenium – a period of 1000 years

minerals – non-living material which occurs naturally in the earth, often in rocks

molten – rock which has been made liquid by great heat

neurotoxic – poisonous or destructive to the nervous system

nocturnal – an animal that is active during the night

nomadic – people who move from place to place seeking new pasture or hunting grounds

nursery herd – a herd of female antelope with young, living together after breeding season

nutrients – natural elements which create richer soil

nymph – the immature stage of some insects

ochre – a yellow, red or brownish mineral made of clay & iron oxide, used as a colouring

omnivorous/omnivore – an animal that eats meat & plants

palatable – grass which is nutritious

perennial – water which lasts all year round

pheromone – a chemical substance released by an animal which affects sexual behaviour

pioneer plant – the first plants to grow in disturbed soil with very little nutrients

plumage – a bird's feathers, particularly in breeding season

predator – an animal (carnivore) that hunts & kills other creatures for food

primate – a specific type of mammal e.g. monkey, baboon

proboscis – elongated mouth part of some insects, used for sucking

quarantined – to isolate animals that may be infected with disease

reservoir – a source of water

rhizome – a modified stem that grows horizontally underground, sending out roots and shoots

rift – a deep crack in the earth

ring-bark – to cut the bark right around the tree eventually killing it

riverine – an area beside a river

where the trees are usually evergreen & dense thickets grow

rodent – a small mammal that only has cutting teeth & usually lives on plants

roost – a place where birds perch or settle to sleep

sanctuary – an area where wildlife is protected

scent-mark – the way in which animals mark their territories using urine, spray or dung

scrotum – the pouch in a male mammal containing the testes

silting up – when fine particles of solid matter build up in water & block the flow of water

smelted – the heating and melting of rock so as to obtain the metal inside

solitary – an animal that generally chooses to live alone

subcontinent – a large landmass like southern Africa that forms part of the whole continent

succulent – juicy plants that contain a lot of moisture

tandem – a situation where animals arrange themselves, one behind the other

tanning – to treat the hide of an animal & convert it into leather

territorial – an animal that defends a particular area against rivals of its own species (usually the same sex)

toxin – a poisonous substance

trance – a dream-like state

translocation – the moving of animals from one area or park to another

transpiration – the act of giving off watery vapour from the surface of leaves

turbulence – a state of unrest

ultraviolet rays – certain rays of the sun that are harmful to the skin & eyes

veterinary control – the control & treatment of animal diseases by a skilled vet

waterlogged – areas that become soaked with water after good rains

weir – a small dam built across a stream or river, so that water-flow can be controlled

SPECIES TICK LIST

The following grids are for you to tick off your discoveries of plants, birds, mammals, reptiles and insects. These have been set out with four columns so that you can keep separate counts on different days, different seasons, different trips.

Page No.	TREES				
51	African Olive				
49	African-wattle				
47	Aloe, Mountain				
57	Broad-pod Elephant-root				
51	Black-thorn Acacia				
50	Buffalo-thorn				
53	Bushveld Red-balloon				
48	Bushveld Shepherds-tree				
47	Bushwillow, Large-fruit				
48	Leadwood				
47	Red				
56	River				
47	Velvet-leaved				
55	Cabbage-tree, Common				
54	Fig, Large-leaved Rock				
53	Highveld Protea				
50	Jacket-plum				
50	Karee				
52	Lavender Croton				
46	Live-long Lannea				
49	Marula				
55	Moepel Red-milkwood				
54	Naboom				
51	Puzzle-bush Stamperwood				
48	Sweet-thorn Acacia				
57	Tamboti				
49	Umbrella Acacia				
51	Weeping Faurea				
52	Wild-pear Dombeya				

	SHRUBS				
46	Black-jack				
52	Fern, Hard				
47	Khaki Weed				
54	Mother-in-law's Tongue				
46	Nightshade				
51	Num-num, Forest				
55	Raisin Bush				
55	Resurrection Plant				
51	Spike-thorn, Kraal				

Page No.	MAMMALS				
22	Aardvark				
22	Aardwolf				
18	Antelope, Sable				
21	Baboon, Chacma				
23	Badger, Honey				
13	Buffalo				
23	Bushbaby, Lesser				
16	Bushbuck				
20	Bushpig				
14	Caracal				
14	Cheetah				
23	Civet, African				
20	Dassie, Rock				
17	Duiker, Common				
16	Eland				
13	Elephant				
19	Gemsbok				
22	Genet, Large-spotted				
13	Giraffe				
22	Hare, Scrub				
18	Hartebeest, Red				
12	Hippopotamus				
14	Hyaena, Brown				
17	Impala				
14	Jackal, Black-backed				
17	Klipspringer				
17	Kudu				
14	Leopard				
14	Lion				
21	Mongoose, Slender				
21	Monkey, Vervet				
23	Pangolin				
23	Porcupine				
22	Rabbit, Smith's Red Rock				
19	Reedbuck, Common				
19	Mountain				
12	Rhinoceros, Black				
12	White				
17	Springbok				
21	Squirrel, Tree				
16	Steenbok				
18	Tssessebe				
20	Warthog				
18	Waterbuck, Common				
14	Wild Cat				
14	Wild Dog				
19	Wildebeest, Blue				
19	Zebra, Plains				

INDEX